NON-LIVING RESOURCES
OF THE CONTINENTAL SHELF
BEYOND 200 NAUTICAL MILES: SPECULATIONS
ON THE IMPLEMENTATION OF
ARTICLE 82 OF THE UNITED NATIONS CONVENTION
ON THE LAW OF THE SEA

ISA TECHNICAL STUDY SERIES

Technical Study No. 1

Global Non-Living Resources on the Extended Continental Shelf: Prospects at the year 2000.

Technical Study No. 2

Polymetallic Massive Sulphides and Cobalt-Rich Ferromanganese Crusts: Status and Prospects.

Technical Study No. 3

Biodiversity, Species Ranges and Gene Flow in the Abyssal Pacific Nodule Province: Predicting and Managing the Impacts of Deep Seabed Mining.

Technical Study No. 4

Issues associated with the Implementation of Article 82 of the United Nations Convention on the Law of the Sea.

NON-LIVING RESOURCES
OF THE CONTINENTAL SHELF BEYOND
200 NAUTICAL MILES: SPECULATIONS
ON THE IMPLEMENTATION OF
ARTICLE 82 OF THE UNITED NATIONS
CONVENTION ON THE LAW OF THE SEA

ISA TECHNICAL STUDY: NO. 5

International Seabed Authority
Kingston, Jamaica

National Library of Jamaica Cataloguing In Publication Data

International Seabed Authority
    Non-living resources of the Continental Shelf beyond 200 nautical miles: speculations on the implementation of article 82 of the United Nations Convention on the Law of the Sea
        p. ; ill. , maps;   cm. – (ISA technical study; no.5)
    Bibliography.
    ISBN: 978-976-95268-1-5 (pkb)
    1. Ocean bottom – Law and legislation. 2. United Nations Convention on the Law of the Sea 3. Maritime law – International cooperation.
    I. Series
    341.455 – dc 22

Copyright © International Seabed Authority 2010

International Seabed Authority
14-20 Port Royal Street
Kingston, Jamaica
Tel: (876) 9229105, Fax: (876) 9220195
URL: http://www.isa.org.jm

TABLE OF CONTENTS

GLOSSARY AND LIST OF ABBREVIATIONS

Authority (the)	International Seabed Authority
CLCS	Commission on the Limits of the Continental Shelf
Continental shelf (geoscientific)	The shallow water (generally less than 200m) platform which forms the perimeter to a continental land mass
Continental shelf (LOSC)	The legal definition provided by the United Nations Convention on the Law of the Sea (LOSC) is that the continental shelf of a coastal State comprises the seabed and subsoil of the submarine areas that extend beyond its territorial sea throughout the natural prolongation of its land territory to the outer edge of the continental margin (Article 76 of LOSC expands this definition further in its paragraphs 1 and 3).
DOALOS	Division for Ocean Affairs and the Law of the Sea
EEZ	Exclusive Economic Zone
GDP	Gross Domestic Product
IMF	International Monetary Fund
ISA	International Seabed Authority (also the Authority)
LOS Convention	1982 United Nations Convention on the Law of the Sea (also LOSC)
Mineral	A naturally occurring solid formed through geological processes that has a characteristic chemical composition, a highly ordered atomic structure, and specific physical properties.
M	Nautical mile
MAR	Mid-Atlantic Ridge
NGDC	National Geophysical Data Center, United States of America
NOCS	National Oceanography Centre, Southampton
OCS	Outer Continental Shelf
OPEC	Organization of the Petroleum Exporting Countries

LIST OF FIGURES AND TABLES

FOREWORD

The 1982 UN Convention on the Law of the Sea (the Convention) is the most important international regime governing the oceans. It covers a wide range of issues, including navigational rights, protection of the marine environment and, relevant for this paper, jurisdiction over living and non-living marine resources. The Convention entered into force in 1994 and, as of October 2009, 158 States and the European Community were parties to the Convention. Of the major powers, only the United States has yet to accede to the Convention, though there are indications it may soon join as well.

The negotiations leading up to the adoption of the Convention were long and complex. One particularly debated topic was the extent of a coastal State's continental shelf. This was eventually set at up to 200 nautical miles from its coastline. However, through a complex assessment mechanism the continental shelf can be extended up to a total of 350 nautical miles from the coastline if the coastal State can show that 'the natural prolongation of its submerged land territory to the outer edge of its continental margin extends beyond the 200-nautical-mile distance criterion.' The area between the 200 nautical miles limit and the border of the total claim is called the Outer Continental Shelf (OCS).

The resources that occur on the world's continental margins may include oil, natural gas, gas hydrates, manganese nodules, sand, gravel, titanium, thorium, iron, nickel, copper, cobalt, gold and diamonds. The size and value of these deposits is unknown, but potential OCS claims cover a large section of the seabed. For comparison, OCS claims could be in excess of 15 million square kilometres, while the world's exclusive economic zones (the water column within 200 nautical miles of the coast) are estimated at approximately 85 million square kilometres, and the Area consists of around 260 million square kilometres.

According to the provisions of the Convention, States wishing to claim an OCS, are required to submit particulars of the claim within ten years of the date of their ratification of the Convention. Because of the difficulty for many States that had ratified the Convention several years ago in complying with that deadline, the Meeting of States Parties to the Convention had agreed that States that ratified the Convention before 13 May 1999 would be permitted to submit their claims by 13 May 2009. As of that date, 51 full submissions to OCS areas and 44 preliminary submissions had been made by more than 70 States. Only about fifteen of these States do not have developing-country status. For many of these developing nations, the added areas of seabed could be economically critical. In particular, land-poor countries such as Barbados, Tonga and Palau are hoping to help secure their financial future with underwater resources.

Sections of the ocean floor that are not part of a territorial claim are called the Area. The mineral resources of the Area are considered a common heritage of mankind and, as a result, those who exploit it have to pay fees for their licences and activities in the Area. That revenue is globally apportioned, with particular emphasis on the needs of developing countries and land-locked States (since the latter have no other way to benefit from marine resources). The International Seabed Authority (the Authority), an intergovernmental organization established by the Convention, was specifically established to act on behalf of humankind in the Area and is tasked with the organization and control of activities in the Area.

The potential extension of coastal States' continental shelves to 350 nautical miles erodes the size of the Area – and hence the resources available to developing and land-locked States. Article 82 of the Convention, which is the subject matter of the present technical study, was introduced as a quid pro quo for this. Article 82 is a unique provision in international law. Motivated by a sense of fairness, it establishes an international 'servitude' in the form of a 'royalty' consisting of payments and contributions to be made by the coastal State to the Authority for the exploitation of the non-living resources of the OCS. There are very few, if any, similar provisions in any other legal instrument which set out a legal obligation designed to address international inequity in a practical way, not simply as a political aspiration or in vague general terms. However Article 82 carries many ambiguities and uncertainties, in part because of its novelty, the difficult compromise behind it and unanswered questions about the mechanisms of implementation.

Responsibility for the implementation of Article 82 rests with the Authority and with States that exploit the non-living resources of their OCS. Payments and contributions are to be made annually by the OCS State at the rate of 1% on the value or volume of all production, commencing on the sixth year of production, increasing by 1% per year until the rate reaches 7% on by the twelfth year, and thereafter remaining at 7%. The Authority then disburses those payments and contributions to State parties 'on the basis of equitable sharing criteria, taking into account the interests and needs of developing States, particularly the least developed and the land-locked among them.'

Although Article 82 has been dormant since the adoption of the Convention, there are coastal States, in particular Canada (which is a State Party to the Convention) and the United States (which is not yet), that have granted prospecting and/or exploration licences or leases on their OCS. Typically, offshore petroleum and mineral development operates on a timeframe that can span decades. Today's prospecting and exploration licence may become a development and production licence within perhaps 10–20 years of initial activity. However, it is possible that Article 82 revenues will come due as soon as 2015. Either way, Article 82 will soon awaken.

However, Article 82 is also a complex provision. It is also the only provision in the Convention setting out an international royalty concerning an activity within national jurisdiction. It contains a rough and untested formula to determine payments or contributions. The uniqueness and complexity of Article 82 demand careful consideration of the obligation, principles and criteria for distribution of benefits, procedural aspects, the role of the Authority, the role of OCS States, and economic and temporal issues.

The Convention provides little guidance to the Authority on how Article 82 might be implemented. Accordingly, one major issue for the Authority is to determine the full extent of its mandate and related powers and functions as it discharges its Article 82 responsibilities. For example, the Council (the executive organ of the Authority comprising 36 elected States) is tasked with recommending to the Assembly (the political body of all 159 members) rules, regulations and procedures on the equitable sharing of financial and other economic benefits made by virtue of Article 82, taking into account the interest and needs of developing States and peoples who have not attained full independence. However, the Article 82 text concerning distribution of payments and contributions suffers from ambiguity. Presumably 'taking into account' implies preferential consideration. What may be intended by 'interests and needs,' and according to whom, is not clear. For example, are developing States with basic livelihood needs on a par with developing States that wish to reduce their dependence on imported energy? Drawing upon existing indices, the Authority may need to develop another composite hierarchy of needs index to rank potential beneficiary States and peoples with reference to the objects and purposes of Article 82.

To begin to answer these, and other, questions around the interpretation and application of Article 82, the Authority, in conjunction with the Energy, Environment and Development Programme of the Royal Institute of International Affairs (Chatham House) in the United Kingdom, convened a seminar for a group of invited experts to discuss the issues associated with Article 82. Chatham House is one of the world's leading organizations for the analysis of international issues. It is membership-based and aims to help individuals and organizations to be at the forefront of developments in an ever-changing and increasingly complex world. The seminar was hosted by Chatham House in London from 11 – 13 February 2009. It was attended by a broad selection of leading academic and practitioner experts in the international law of the sea, marine geology and oceanography, as well as the offshore oil and gas industry from Europe, Africa, Asia, and North and South America (the list of participants appears in Annex III).

Discussions at the seminar were assisted by two working papers commissioned by the Authority. The first paper, prepared by Dr Aldo Chircop of Dalhousie University, Canada, presented a study of issues associated with the implementation of Article 82 from a legal and policy perspective. The second paper, prepared by Dr Lindsay Parson of the National Oceanography Centre, Southampton, UK, provided a technical overview of the current status of OCS claims and the resource potential of OCS areas.

The present report is a revised version of Dr Parson's paper. Following the seminar, the paper was extensively revised to take into account the views expressed by participants in the seminar and to try to reflect the thoughts of participants as to the status and prospects of non-living resources in the outer continental shelf. The Authority is extremely grateful to Dr Parson not only for his original report, but also for the many hours spent in working with the legal and technical staff of the Authority in revising the document in light of the discussions at Chatham House. In accordance with the Chatham House Rule, none of the views expressed at the seminar are attributed in this report to any particular individual or organization, including the Authority. The report is intended to have no status other than as a transparent and exhaustive study of the issues associated with the delineation of the outer limits of the continental shelf worldwide and speculations on the prospects for exploitation of non-living resources in these areas, compiled with the benefit of the views of some of the very best experts available.

The associated technical report by Dr Chircop has already been published by the Authority as Technical Study No. 4.

The key conclusions from this report are threefold. First, it is clear that the process of delineating the limits of the continental shelf is well underway; but the time frame within which this process will be concluded is highly uncertain. Second, there is no doubt that the potential outer continental shelf areas harbour extensive reservoirs of non-living resources, including some, such as methane hydrates, which are relatively unexplored but may offer vast future potential. Third, given the likely length of time it will take for States not only to delineate their outer continental shelf areas, but also to establish licensing regimes for these areas, it should not be expected that revenue flows under Article 82 will commence before 2015 at the earliest.

In many ways these conclusions complement the core recommendation of the companion study of the legal and policy issues associated with the implementation of Article 82, namely that the Authority will need to develop a strategy for bringing Article 82 to the attention of Member States and to explore a practical approach to its implementation. This is most easily, and appropriately, done while the provision is still dormant, especially as its implementation has both international and domestic implications.

The Authority's work in relation to Article 82 is just beginning. Already, at the fifteenth session of the Authority, held in Kingston, Jamaica, in May 2009, Member States expressed interest in the outcomes of the Chatham House seminar and requested the Secretary-General to consider including matters relating to the implementation of Article 82 in the next programme of work for the Authority. It is hoped that the present report, combined with its companion study, will provide a solid factual background for Member States, whether OCS States or potential beneficiary States, to embark upon what is likely to be a long and detailed discussion of all the issues associated with Article 82 and its implementation.

Finally, the Authority wishes to express its appreciation to Chatham House and in particular the staff of the Energy, Environment and Development Programme, for their cooperation and enthusiasm for this project.

EXECUTIVE SUMMARY

Article 82 of the United Nations Convention on the Law of the Sea provides for a system of revenue sharing by means of payments or contributions in kind with respect to the production of non-living resources of the continental shelf lying beyond 200 nautical miles. The establishment of the outer limits of continental shelf of the world's coastal States is undertaken according to Article 76 of the Convention, and this is well underway, although the Commission on the Limits of the Continental Shelf, which was set up to oversee the process, warns that decades may pass before the task is complete. This study reviews the types of resources that may occur in these areas of outer continental shelf, comments on their accessibility (both in terms of their location and the technology available for exploration and extraction), and speculates on the development of licencing systems for areas of resource potential which straddle different operational regimes. Taking into account the rate of delivery of recommendations of the Commission with regard to continental shelf limits, specific observations are made on the likely schedule of first payments by coastal States according to the provisions of Article 82. Even if those States that have completed their outer shelf delimitation move to set up exploration and extraction measures immediately, the five year 'grace period' in production allowed before revenue is required under Article 82 is unlikely to finish before the end of the decade. Furthermore, the rate of completion of new recommendations by the Commission indicates a slow start to the revenue flow from the provisions laid out in Article 82.

1. ARTICLE 82 AND ITS CONTEXT IN PART VI OF THE CONVENTION

Part VI (Articles 76 to 85) and Annex II of the United Nations Convention on the Law of the Sea[1] (hereafter referred to as 'the LOS Convention' or 'LOSC') define the continental shelf, the methods to establish its limits and the rights and obligations incumbent upon the coastal States in respect of the continental shelf and its sedentary species, its minerals and other non-living resources.

1.1 Article 82 from the perspective of the continental shelf

1.1.1   Article 82 is one of the special provisions (along with Article 76, paragraphs 4 to 8 in Part VI of the Convention and Annex II) that applies only where the continental shelf extends beyond 200 nautical miles (M). However, the implementation of Article 82 does not depend on the establishment of the outer limits of the continental shelf. This is no coincidence, since Articles 76 and 82 encapsulate the compromise on the definition of the continental shelf in the Convention. Indeed, the relationship between Article 76 and Article 82 is rooted in the protracted and intricate negotiations on the continental shelf during the Third United Nations Conference on the Law of the Sea (UNCLOS III). Article 82 designed a mechanism for revenue sharing derived from the exploitation of the non-living resources of the continental margin beyond 200M as a quid pro quo in exchange for recognition of the entitlement to the continental shelf beyond 200M.

1.2 Scope of the analysis

1.2.1   Article 82 of the Convention has no equivalent provision in international law. This most innovatory provision requires States to make payments or contributions in kind with respect to the exploitation of the non-living resources in the continental shelf beyond 200M. Developing States that are net importers of the particular mineral

---

[1]   *United Nations Convention on the Law of the Sea*, Montego Bay, 10 December 1982, 1833 UNTS 3. A consolidated version of the LOS Convention and other accompanying basic texts are reproduced in *The Law of the Sea: Compendium of Basic Documents* (Kingston, Jamaica: International Seabed Authority & Caribbean Law Publishing Co., 2001). In addition, the Third United Nations Conference on the Law of the Sea adopted on 29 August 1980 to include as Annex II to the Final Act of the Convention a "Statement of Understanding" concerning a specific method applicable to special geological and geomorphological characteristics such as those in the southern part of the Bay of Bengal.

resources produced from their continental shelves are released from this obligation in respect of those mineral resources.

1.2.2   Payments and contributions are made on an annual basis at the rate of 1 per cent on the value or volume of all production, beginning on the sixth year of production. Then the rate will augment annually by one per cent, to remain at 7 per cent after the twelfth year. Resources used in relation to exploitation are not deemed part of production. The payments and contributions are channelled through the International Seabed Authority. Article 82 entrusts the Authority with the distribution of payments and contributions to States Parties according to equitable criteria, taking into account the interests and needs of developing States, and especially the least developed and landlocked States, as well as peoples who have not yet achieved full independence or other self-governing status.

1.2.3   Article 82 refers to the exploitation of non-living resources of the continental shelf, whereas the development of the continental shelf had previously been limited to its fishery resources. Article 82 therefore presupposes the economic potential of non-living resources resulting from the geological formation of the continental margin. A range of mineral resources have been identified as characteristic of continental shelf areas. These deposits are found locally extending beyond 200M and into the outer continental shelf (OCS). Some, such as polymetallic nodules, are found in the deepest waters and predominantly at lower latitudes, but others, such as cobalt crusts, are more widely distributed. Other mineral deposits, such as methane hydrates, are more common along continental margins while polymetallic sulphides are formed at actively spreading ocean ridge systems.[2]

1.2.4   The presence of mineral resources such as polymetallic nodules and hydrocarbons can be explained by the extension of continental geological settings and the accumulation of sediments from continents rich in minerals and organic compounds. Most hydrocarbon resources are estimated to be found between the coastline and the foot of the continental slope, whereas much smaller quantities seem to lie on the abyssal plains, ocean trenches and ridges, where their exploitation is extremely difficult. The variety, abundance and net value of these resources are poorly understood, although workable estimates of these parameters can be provided by models calibrated by sampling and surveying. The practicalities of recovering, processing and marketing the resources are discussed below.

1.2.5   The principal focus of this report is twofold: (a) to identify the potential value of resources to which Article 82 applies, and (b) to discuss the feasibility of recovering those resources and to speculate on the timescale in which the revenue collection process under Article 82 may be expected to come into operation. With regard to the latter, it is worth bearing in mind that some coastal States have already granted prospecting and/or hydrocarbon exploration licenses or leases on their continental shelf

---

[2]   A synthesis of all mineral deposits likely to occur in shelf environments is given in, International Seabed Authority, *Global Non-Living Resources On The Extended Continental Shelf: Prospects at the Year 2000*, Technical Study No.1, Kingston, ISA (2001).

beyond 200M,[3] and there are reports of coastal States that have received requests for licences to extract other, non-hydrocarbon mineral resources.[4]

1.2.6   The English text of Article 82 states:

Payments and contributions with respect to the exploitation of the continental shelf beyond 200 nautical miles

1   The coastal State shall make payments or contributions in kind in respect of the exploitation of the non-living resources of the continental shelf beyond 200 nautical miles from the baselines from which the breadth of the territorial sea is measured.

2   The payments and contributions shall be made annually with respect to all production at a site after the first five years of production at that site. For the sixth year, the rate of payment or contribution shall be 1 per cent of the value or volume of production at the site. The rate shall increase by 1 per cent for each subsequent year until the twelfth year and shall remain at 7 per cent thereafter. Production does not include resources used in connection with exploitation.

3   A developing State which is a net importer of a mineral resource produced from its continental shelf is exempt from making such payments or contributions in respect of that mineral resource.

4   The payments or contributions shall be made through the Authority, which shall distribute them to States Parties to this Convention, on the basis of equitable sharing criteria, taking into account the interests and needs of developing States, particularly the least developed and the land-locked among them.

---

[3]   International Seabed Authority, *Issues associated with the Implementation of Article 82 of the United Nations Convention on the Law of the Sea*, Technical Study No. 4, Kingston, ISA (2009).

[4]   Pers. Comm., Kaiser de Souza (2009), referring to a Brazilian coral extraction contractor seeking to recover deposits from areas beyond 200 nautical miles on the Brazilian shelf, between mainland and the Trindade and Martim Vaz Island Groups.

2. RELATIONSHIP OF ARTICLE 82 WITH OTHER ARTICLES IN PART VI OF THE CONVENTION

Article 82 is one of the 10 articles contained in Part VI of the Convention dealing with the continental shelf, its definition and the rights and obligations of States. In this section, Article 82 is discussed in the context of the legal definition of the continental shelf, and with its legal regime.

2.1 Article 82 and the legal definition of the continental shelf

2.1.1   Article 82 does not apply to the entire continental shelf but only to the portion of continental shelves that extend beyond 200M. Article 76 provides the legal definition of the continental shelf, and the methods for the establishment of the outer limits of the continental shelf where it lies beyond 200M, provided the appropriate seafloor morphology and/or geological conditions are met. Article 76 comprises 10 paragraphs and the English text states:

Definition of the continental shelf

1   *The continental shelf of a coastal State comprises the seabed and subsoil of the submarine areas that extend beyond its territorial sea throughout the natural prolongation of its land territory to the outer edge of the continental margin, or to a distance of 200 nautical miles from the baselines from which the breadth of the territorial sea is measured where the outer edge of the continental margin does not extend up to that distance.*

2   *The continental shelf of a coastal State shall not extend beyond the limits provided for in paragraphs 4 to 6.*

3   *The continental margin comprises the submerged prolongation of the land mass of the coastal State, and consists of the seabed and subsoil of the shelf, the slope and the rise. It does not include the deep ocean floor with its oceanic ridges or the subsoil thereof.*

4   *(a) For the purposes of this Convention, the coastal State shall establish the outer edge of the continental margin wherever the margin extends beyond 200 nautical miles from the baselines from which the breadth of the territorial sea is measured, by either:*

   (i) a line delineated in accordance with paragraph 7 by reference to the outermost fixed points at each of which the thickness of sedimentary rocks is at least 1 per cent of the shortest distance from such point to the foot of the continental slope; or

   (ii) a line delineated in accordance with paragraph 7 by reference to fixed points not more than 60 nautical miles from the foot of the continental slope.

(b)   In the absence of evidence to the contrary, the foot of the continental slope shall be determined as the point of maximum change in the gradient at its base.

5   *The fixed points comprising the line of the outer limits of the continental shelf on the seabed, drawn in accordance with paragraph 4 (a)(i) and (ii), either shall not exceed 350 nautical miles from the baselines from which the breadth of the territorial sea is measured or shall not exceed 100 nautical miles from the 2,500 metre isobath, which is a line connecting the depth of 2,500 metres.*

6   *Notwithstanding the provisions of paragraph 5, on submarine ridges, the outer limit of the continental shelf shall not exceed 350 nautical miles from the baselines from which the breadth of the territorial sea is measured. This paragraph does not apply to submarine elevations that are natural components of the continental margin, such as its plateaux, rises, caps, banks and spurs.*

7   *The coastal State shall delineate the outer limits of its continental shelf, where that shelf extends beyond 200 nautical miles from the baselines from which the breadth of the territorial sea is measured, by straight lines not exceeding 60 nautical miles in length, connecting fixed points, defined by co-ordinates of latitude and longitude.*

8   *Information on the limits of the continental shelf beyond 200 nautical miles from the baselines from which the breadth of the territorial sea is measured shall be submitted by the coastal State to the Commission on the Limits of the Continental Shelf set up under Annex II on the basis of equitable geographical representation. The Commission shall make recommendations to coastal States on matters related to the establishment of the outer limits of their continental shelf. The limits of the shelf established by a coastal State on the basis of these recommendations shall be final and binding.*

9   *The coastal State shall deposit with the Secretary-General of the United Nations charts and relevant information, including geodetic data, permanently describing the outer limits of its continental shelf. The Secretary-General shall give due publicity thereto.*

10 *The provisions of this article are without prejudice to the question of delimitation of the continental shelf between States with opposite or adjacent coasts.*

2.1.2   Paragraph 1 determines that the continental shelf is comprised of the seabed and subsoil beyond the outer limits of the territorial sea throughout the natural prolongation of its land territory. The extent of the continental shelf corresponds to the natural prolongation of the land territory of a coastal State up to the outer edge of the continental margin, or up to an arbitrary distance of 200M, where the outer edge of the continental margin does not reach 200M. Thus, the first element is based on geomorphological considerations and implies the determination of the outer edge of the continental margin. The second element is based on a distance criterion, which emphasizes that regardless of the geology or the geomorphology of the seabed and subsoil, the continental shelf of a coastal State extends to 200M, which also coincides with the maximum extent of the exclusive economic zone (EEZ); where the continental shelf does not extend beyond 200M, therefore, Article 82 is not applicable.

2.1.3   Paragraph 2 indicates that there are maximum seaward limits of the continental shelf, which are described in paragraphs 4 to 6.

2.1.4   Paragraph 3 defines the continental margin, which consists of the submerged prolongation of the land mass of the coastal State and includes the seabed and subsoil of the shelf, the slope and the rise, but not the deep ocean floor with its oceanic ridges or the subsoil thereof.

2.1.5   Paragraphs 4 to 7 apply terms and methods for the establishment of the outer limits of the legal continental shelf (margin) beyond 200M from the baselines. The coastal State establishes the outer edge of the continental margin by straight lines not exceeding 60M long between connecting points (paragraph 7). These points are established in two ways, as provided in paragraph 4(a) (i) and (ii). According to the first method, the outermost fixed points of the continental margin are located where the ratio of thickness of sedimentary rocks to distance from foot of slope corresponds to at least 1:100. In accordance with the second method, the outermost fixed points delineating the outer edge of the continental margin must not be located more than 60M from the foot of the continental slope. Both of those methods require the determination of the foot of the slope. Paragraph 4 (b) describes the foot of the slope as the point of maximum change at the base of the slope, except where it is determined by evidence to the contrary.

2.1.6   Whichever method applies, paragraph 5 introduces two limits, or constraints, to the fixation of the outermost points. They must not be further than 100M beyond the 2,500 metre isobath (the depth constraint) or more than 350M from the baselines of the coast (the distance constraint). Any combination of these two constraints can be utilised to optimise the position of the outer limit so as to maximise the area of the shelf. As provided in paragraph 6, in the case of submarine ridges, the 350M cut-off is applicable if such ridges are not submarine elevations, that is, natural components of the continental margin, for example its plateaux, rises, caps, banks and spurs.

2.1.7   By involving an international technical body, the establishment of the outer limits of the continental shelf differs from the establishment of the seaward limit of other coastal State zones. Paragraph 8 sets up the Commission on the Limits of the Continental Shelf (CLCS) with a mandate to make recommendations to coastal States concerning the establishment of the outer limits of their continental shelf. Based on such recommendations, coastal States establish the outer limits of their continental shelves, which are final and binding. The Commission was established in 1997 and has completed consideration of nine of the 51 submissions from coastal States received as of 31 January 2010.

2.1.8   Paragraph 9 sets out the functions of the Secretary-General of the United Nations with respect to giving due publicity to the deposition of charts and relevant information, including geodetic data, which permanently describe the outer limits of coastal States' continental shelves. It is essential for the international community to know the extent of national jurisdiction, both for the implementation of the provisions of Article 82 and for the administration of the Area by the International Seabed Authority. On 20 May 2009 and 19 August 2009, respectively, Mexico (in respect of the western polygon in the Gulf of Mexico) and Ireland (with respect to the area abutting the Porcupine Abyssal Plain) became the first two States to have fulfilled their obligations to deposit this information.[5]

2.1.9   Paragraph 10 stipulates that the provisions of Article 76 are without prejudice to the question of the delimitation of the continental shelf between States with opposite or adjacent coasts. This confirms that Article 76 addresses the entitlement to and the establishment of the outer limits of the continental shelf but not the question of overlapping delimitations.

2.1.10   Of the 159 States that had ratified the Convention as of 31 January 2010, it is likely that between 60 and 70 have a continental shelf which has the potential to extend beyond 200M. It will fall to the CLCS to decide whether these States have provided sufficient, good quality data and analyses in support of their submissions. The number of submissions to be examined by the Commission is considerable. In reality, however, there may be even more, as for a variety of reasons; several States have already declared that they will be delivering their continental shelf arguments and materials as a number of separate, partial submissions. As a result, the final number of submissions to be examined by the Commission will inevitably be much higher – perhaps as many as 100.

2.1.11   According to the provisions of Article 4 of Annex II of the Convention, a coastal State is required to submit particulars of the outer limits of its continental shelf to the Commission within 10 years of the date of its expression of consent to be bound by the Convention. After much deliberation by the States Parties to the Convention, as well as the recognition of the difficulties encountered by (among others) developing and Small Island States in preparing submissions, the eleventh Meeting of States Parties to the Convention decided[6] that in the case of a State Party for which the Convention entered into force before 13 May 1999, the calculation of the 10-year period will commence on 13 May 1999, this being the date of the publication of the Scientific and Technical Guidelines of the Commission on the Limits of the Continental Shelf (CLCS/11, 1999).

2.1.12   Additional variations in submission procedures were provided at the eighteenth Meeting of States Parties to the Convention, when the continuing difficulties experienced by certain States in fulfilling the requirements of Article 4 of Annex II of the

---

[5]   M.Z.N. 72. 2009. LOS of 8 June 2009, Deposit by Mexico, pursuant to Article 76, paragraph 9, of the Convention, of a chart and relevant information, including geodetic data, permanently describing the outer limits of its continental shelf beyond 200 nautical miles from the baselines from which the breadth of the territorial sea is measured in respect of the western polygon in the Gulf of Mexico; M.Z.N. 73. 2009. LOS of 26 October 2009, Deposit pursuant to Article 76, paragraph 9, of the Convention of a list of geographical coordinates of points, including geodetic datum, accompanied by an illustrative map, permanently describing the outer limits of its continental shelf beyond 200 nautical miles from the baselines from which the breadth of the territorial sea of Ireland is measured in the area abutting the Porcupine Abyssal Plain. See http://www.un.org/Depts/los/LEGISLATIONANDTREATIES/depositpublicity.htm.

[6]   SPLOS/72, 2001.

Convention were recognised. These difficulties were seen to be affecting, in particular, developing countries and Small Island Developing States. The Meeting of States Parties to the Convention decided accordingly that the requirements of Article 4 of Annex II of the Convention would be satisfied by submission to the Secretary-General of the United Nations of preliminary information indicative of the outer limits of the continental shelf beyond 200M, along with a description of the status of preparation and intended date of making a full submission in accordance with Article 76 and the Rules of Procedure of the Commission. This decision was taken on 28 June 2008 (SPLOS/183, 2008).

   2.1.13   By 31 January 2010, the CLCS had received 51 submissions in respect of coastal States' continental shelf areas beyond 200M from, in the order of receipt: the Russian Federation; Brazil; Australia; Ireland (Porcupine Abyssal Plain); New Zealand; joint submission by France, Ireland, Spain and the United Kingdom of Great Britain and Northern Ireland (United Kingdom) (Celtic Sea and Bay of Biscay); Norway (the North East Atlantic and Arctic); France (areas of French Guiana and New Caledonia); Mexico (western polygon in the Gulf of Mexico); Barbados; United Kingdom (Ascension Island); Indonesia (north west of Sumatra Island); Japan; joint submission by Mauritius and the Seychelles (Mascarene Plateau); Suriname; Myanmar; France (French Antilles and Kerguelen Islands); Yemen (south east of Socotra Island); United Kingdom (Hatton Rockall Area); Ireland (Hatton Rockall Area); Uruguay; Philippines (Benham Rise region); the Cook Islands (the Manihiki Plateau); Fiji; Argentina; Ghana; Iceland (Ægir Basin area and western and southern parts of Reykjanes Ridge); Denmark (the area north of the Faroe Islands); Pakistan; Norway (Bouvetøya and Dronning Maud Land); South Africa (the mainland of the territory of South Africa); joint submission by the Federated States of Micronesia, Papua New Guinea and Solomon Islands (Ontong Java Plateau); joint submission by Malaysia and Viet Nam (southern South China Sea); joint submission by France and South Africa (Crozet Archipelago and the Prince Edward Islands); Kenya; Mauritius (Rodrigues Island); Viet Nam (North Area, VNM-N); Nigeria; Seychelles (Northern Plateau Region); France (La Réunion Island and Saint-Paul and Amsterdam Islands); Palau; Côte d'Ivoire; Sri Lanka; Portugal; United Kingdom (Falkland Islands, South Georgia and the South Sandwich Islands); Tonga; Spain (Galicia); India; Trinidad and Tobago; Namibia and Cuba.

   2.1.14   In addition to the full and/or partial submissions presented by coastal States, the Secretary-General of the United Nations received before 31 January 2010 a further 44 sets of preliminary indicative information containing a description of the status of preparation and intended date of submission, which satisfied the period referred to in Article 4 of Annex II to the Convention noted above. These came from: Angola; the Bahamas; Benin; Benin and Togo; Brunei Darussalam; Cameroon; Cape Verde; Chile; China; the Comoros; the Congo; Costa Rica; Cuba; Democratic Republic of the Congo; Equatorial Guinea; Fiji; Fiji and Solomon Islands; Fiji and Solomon Islands and Vanuatu; France (French Polynesia and Wallis and Futuna Islands); France (Saint-Pierre-et-Miquelon); Gabon; Gambia; Guinea; Guinea-Bissau; Guyana; Mauritania; Mauritius; Mexico; Federated States of Micronesia (Eauripik Rise region, Mussau Ridge region); Mozambique; New Zealand (Tokelau); Oman; Papua New Guinea (Eauripik Rise region, Mussau Ridge region); the Republic of Korea; Sao Tome and Principe;

Senegal; Seychelles; Sierra Leone; Solomon Islands; Somalia; Spain (west of Canary Islands); Togo; the United Republic of Tanzania and Vanuatu.

2.1.15 A summary chart has recently been published by the National Oceanography Centre, Southampton, UK, which synthesises all submissions made as of 31 January 2010 (see also the explanatory notes to the chart contained in Annex I).[7]

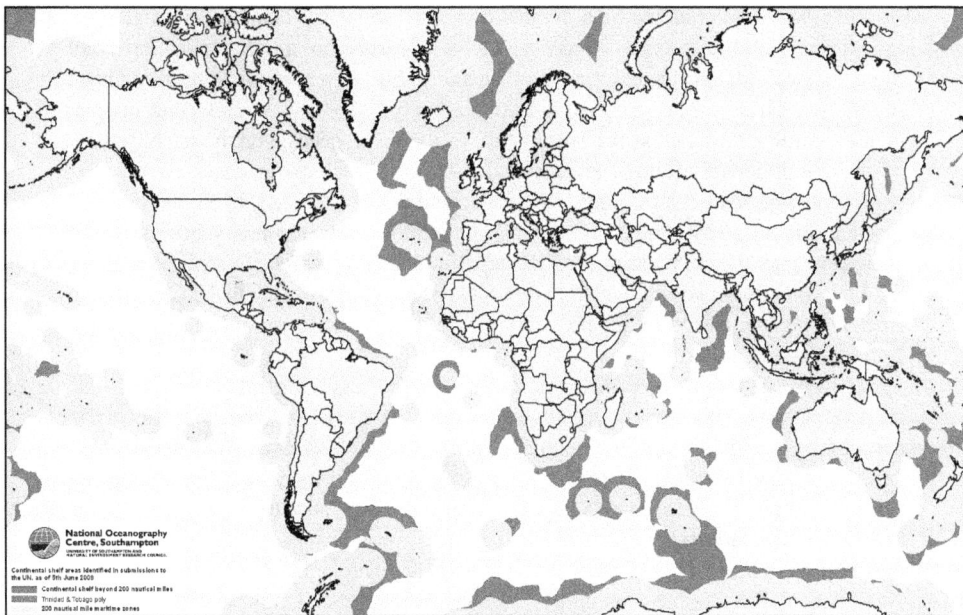

Figure 1. Summary chart of all 200M limits (in pale blue) and areas of OCS relating to submissions made by coastal States up to 31 January 2010 (in red).

2.1.16 The Commission was set up pursuant to Article 76, paragraph 8, and under Annex II to the Convention, on the basis of equitable geographical representation. The Commission is composed of 21 members who are experts in geology, geophysics or hydrography. They are elected by States Parties to the Convention and serve in their personal capacity.

2.1.17 The function of the Commission is twofold: (a) to consider the data and other material submitted by coastal States concerning the outer limits of the continental shelf in areas where those limits extend beyond 200 nautical miles, and to make recommendations in accordance with Article 76 and the Statement of Understanding of 29 August 1980 by the Third United Nations Conference on the Law of the Sea; and (b) to provide scientific and technical advice, if requested by the coastal State concerned during the preparation of the data referred to above (Article 3, paragraph 1, Annex II to the Convention).

---

[7] www.unclosuk.org

2.1.18   The Commission meets twice a year, usually in March/April and August/ September, at the headquarters of the United Nations. Its sessions consist of plenary meetings and periods devoted to the technical review of submissions at the Geographic Information System laboratories and other facilities of the Division for Ocean Affairs and the Law of the Sea (DOALOS). The meetings of the Commission, its subcommissions and subsidiary bodies are in private, unless the Commission decides otherwise (rule 23 of the Rules of Procedure of the Commission (CLCS/40/Rev.1).

2.1.19   Upon receipt of a submission, the Secretary-General circulates, in accordance with the Rules of Procedure of the Commission, a communication to all Member States of the United Nations to make public an executive summary of the submission. The Secretary-General also publicises communications received from other States regarding the submission. Then the Commission proceeds with the establishment of subcommissions made up of seven members for the consideration of each submission. Due to the workload, the Commission has decided that only three subcommissions can function simultaneously. Some members may be members of two or three subcommissions at the same time. The submissions are queued in the order of their receipt. Only after one of the three working subcommissions has presented its recommendations to the Commission will the next submission in line be examined (rule 51 of the Rules of Procedure of the Commission).

2.1.20   There are a number of relevant issues regarding interaction between the Commission and States, including the participation of the coastal State in the proceedings of the Commission, confidentiality, and assistance provided by any member of the Commission to the submitting State. Further, both the submitting coastal State and the States with adjacent or opposite coasts need to communicate to the Commission situations of unresolved land or maritime dispute, and dispute concerning the delimitation of the continental shelf between opposite or adjacent States.

2.1.21   The Commission, through the Secretary-General, notifies the submitting State no later than 60 days prior to the opening date of the session of the day and place where the submission will be first considered. The submitting State, in accordance with Article 5 of Annex II to the Convention, is invited to send its representatives to participate, without the right to vote, in the relevant proceedings of the Commission. The Commission, given the particulars of each submission, has identified three proceedings involving the participation of representatives of the submitting State: (i) in accordance with paragraph 2(a) of section II of the Rules of Procedure, the representatives of the submitting State introduce the submission to the Commission; (ii) the subcommission may then invite the representatives of the submitting State for consultation; and (iii) meetings may be held to clarify any matters relating to the submission.

2.1.22   After the subcommission presents its recommendations to the Commission, and before their consideration and adoption by the Commission, the submitting State may make a presentation on any matter related to its submission to the plenary of the Commission.

2.1.23   Confidentiality of data and information is highly significant to both the submitting State and the Commission. The submitting State may classify as confidential any data or other material in the submission. These remain confidential after the review of the submission unless the Commission, with the written consent of the submitting State, decides otherwise. Annex II to the Rules of Procedure details procedures for access to confidential material.

2.1.24   By 31 January 2010, the Commission had issued recommendations in respect of nine submissions, from: the Russian Federation (27 June 2002); Brazil (4 April 2007); Australia (9 April 2008); Ireland (Porcupine Abyssal Plain, 5 April 2007); New Zealand (22 August 2008); jointly by France, Ireland, Spain and the United Kingdom (Celtic Sea and the Bay of Biscay, 24 March 2009); Norway (Northeast Atlantic and Arctic, 27 March 2009); Mexico (western polygon in the Gulf of Mexico, 31 March 2009); and France (French Guiana and New Caledonia, 2 September 2009).

2.1.25   A recurrent concern of States Parties and others has been the capacity of the Commission to deal with the number of submissions waiting to be considered. During the fifteenth Meeting of States Parties to the Convention in 2005, the Chairman of the Commission, Mr. Peter Croker, revealed that the predicted submissions by an estimated 28 coastal States by the May 2009 deadline would result in an unsustainable workload under the prevailing working practices.[8] During the nineteenth Meeting of States Parties, in the knowledge that 50 submissions had been received by the deadline of 13 May 2009, and one subsequently, the third Chairman of the Commission, Mr. Alexandre Tagore Medeiros de Albuquerque estimated that at the present rate of progress, the latest submissions received would not be considered by subcommissions before August 2028 (during the sixty-second session of the Commission). Recommendations could be issued in respect of the corresponding coastal States no earlier than March 2030 (during the sixty-fifth session of the Commission).[9]

2.1.26   It is clear that a speedy advance towards exploitation on the areas of continental shelf beyond 200M is currently unlikely for late-submitting coastal States awaiting the due process of examination and recommendation by the CLCS. Nonetheless, there is a real need to assess the potential type and value of the resources relevant to these areas of OCS, in order to inform the process. The following paragraphs examine the possible timing of these processes for a selection of coastal States, all of which have already made, or are intending to make, submissions to the Commission.

2.1.27   Estimating which coastal States will be first to exploit their marine resources beyond 200M involves speculation. Factors could include: established and specialised expertise/track record in technology used in deep water exploration and exploitation (for example, Brazil); an inadequate resource base within existing shelf areas (for example, New Zealand); or burgeoning demand due to rapid rise in consumer and commercial development (for example, China and India).[10]

2.1.28   Table 1 (below) focuses on eight coastal States, all of which demonstrate factors that suggest they may be among the first to implement Article 82 provisions.

---

[8]   SPLOS/135, Report of the fifteenth Meeting of States Parties to the Convention, para. 68 (New York, 16-24 June 2005).

[9]   From 'Present scenario of the practical difficulties in view of the increased workload of the Commission on the Limits of the Continental Shelf (CLCS)', presentation made by the Chairman to the nineteenth Meeting of States Parties to the Convention, New York, 19 June 2009.

[10]   To complement these observations, the reader is also referred to the Technical Study No. 4 "Issues associated with the implementation of Article 82 of the United Nations Convention on the Law of the Sea", especially pp. 45-63, and Chapter 6 as a whole.

These factors include the presence of wide, resource-rich shelf areas, and well-developed infrastructures, licensing systems and markets. This exercise uses conventional hydrocarbons as an example. The table shows estimates of the approximate year by which the States will begin to make payments or contributions in kind through the Authority for onward distribution. In addition, and for comparison only, a similar exercise examines the timing of Article 82 provisions and parameters likely to be relevant to the United States of America (USA). While the USA is not a State Party to the Convention, it is expected to become one in the near future, and it is inevitable that, as one of the major oil producers, it may be significantly affected by the revenue sharing provisions outlined in Article 82.

    2.1.29   Table 1 shows estimated dates by which revenue under Article 82 provisions will commence. While purely theoretical these figures represent a reasonable earliest indicative dates. The amount of revenue accrued will be determined by the level of production undertaken, and coastal States' need to exploit the resource. Naturally, it is appropriate that this study focuses on conventional hydrocarbons in making these estimates, but similar tables of expected revenue could theoretically be produced for the known range of mineral resources likely to occur in areas of OCS.

TABLE 1. SUMMARY OF RECENT ANNUAL HYDROCARBON PRODUCTION FOR NINE COASTAL STATES WITH POTENTIAL TO SUCCESSFULLY SECURE EXPLORATION AND EXPLOITATION RIGHTS OVER THEIR OCS (SOURCE: INTERNATIONAL ENERGY AUTHORITY, 2007), AND POSSIBLE TIMING OF INITIAL REVENUE RESULTING FROM IMPLEMENTATION OF ARTICLE 82

Coastal State - year of ratification or accession to UNLOSC in brackets	Current EEZ (Mill sq km)	Potential area of continental shelf beyond 200M (Mill sq km)	Annual hydrocarbon production (a) (Crude oil, Unit: 1,000 tonnes)	Estimated date of establishment of the outer limits of the continental shelf (b)	Estimated date of initial revenue yield under Article 82 (c)	Special factors relating to coastal State
Brazil (1988)	3.66	0.926	89,137	2011 (d)	2017	Leading expertise in deep water production technology
Canada (2003)	2.75	1.3	110,389	2030 (e)	2036	Oil production already mature at 200M

China (1996)	0.74	N/A	186,318	2030 (f)	2036	Rapidly rising demand
Australia (1994)	6.05	3.4	21,559	2009	2015	Multiple OCS potential
New Zealand (1996)	4.08	1.7	1,874	2009	2015	Coastal State with rising demand and modest reserves
Angola (1990)	0.5	0.047	84,908	2011	2017	Resource at deep water, conventional hydrocarbons and gas hydrates (g)
Japan (1996)	4.48	0.75	286	2012	2018	Coastal State with rising demand and modest reserves
India (1995)	2.3	>1.0	34,117	2028	2034	Rapidly rising demand
USA	11.35	>1.0	249,791	2030	2036	Date of accession to the Convention undecided

(a) *International Energy Authority, 2007 figures, see http://www.iea.org/stats.*
(b) *Dates taken from the presentation by the Chairman of the CLCS, Mr Alexandre Tagore Medeiros de Albuquerque "Present scenario of the practical difficulties in view of the increased workload of the Commission on the Limits of the Continental Shelf" (mimeo.), delivered at the nineteenth Meeting of the States Parties, June 2009.*
(c) *Assumes State establishes licencing regime immediately following adoption of recommendations of the CLCS, and initiates production in same year. Revenue as provided for under Article 82 would start in sixth year.*
(d) *Recommendations adopted by the CLCS on the 4th April 2007 reducing original case area. Brazil is preparing additional data to support its original position. This date assumes completion of revised case by 2011.*
(e) *Assumes Canada makes 52nd submission to the CLCS, and uses dates as predicted.*
(f) *Assumes China makes 52nd submission to the CLCS, and uses dates as predicted.*
(g) *See section 4.8, below.*

2.1.30   The table shows likely start dates for the generation of the first revenues under Article 82, based on a lag time of six years following issuance of recommendations by the CLCS, and the probable enactment of appropriate national legislation.

2.2 Article 82 and the legal regime applicable to the continental shelf beyond 200M

2.2.1   This section shows how the implementation of Article 82 of the Convention relates to the continental shelf regime. Article 77 of the Convention provides coastal States with sovereign rights over the continental shelf, for the purpose of exploring and exploiting its natural resources. The sovereign rights of the coastal States over the continental shelf exist *ab initio* and *ipso jure* regardless of the extent of the continental shelf and regardless of the establishment of the outer limits of the continental shelf beyond 200M. They are exclusive and do not depend on effective or notional occupation or on any express proclamation. Therefore, a coastal State is entitled to exercise those rights even before the limits are final and binding. In other words, the extraction of resources from the OCS (which would in turn trigger the implementation of Article 82) is not contingent on the delineation of the outer limits of the continental shelf beyond 200M.

2.2.2   Articles 78, 79, 80, 81 and 85 list specific rights of coastal States concerning other activities on the continental shelf, which can thus take place irrespective of the scope of application of Article 82. By virtue of Article 78, the exercise of sovereign rights by a coastal State are offset with provisions protecting the freedom of navigation and other rights and freedoms of other States from infringement or unjustifiable interference by the coastal State. This applies to the continental shelf on its entire extent, including beyond 200M.

2.2.3   Article 79 provides all States with the right to lay submarine cables and pipelines on the continental shelf, subjecting the delineation of the course for the laying of the pipelines to the consent of the coastal State. Article 80 expands to the continental shelf the rules relating to artificial islands, installations and structures in the EEZ that are set out in Article 60. Article 81 recognizes the exclusive right of the coastal State to authorize and regulate all drilling on the continental shelf, which means for purposes other than the exploration and exploitation of the natural resources under Article 77, paragraph 1. Article 85 states that Part VI of the Convention does not prejudice to the right of the coastal State to exploit the subsoil by means of tunnelling, regardless of the depth of the water above the subsoil. Article 83 addresses the delimitation of overlapping entitlements between neighbouring States with opposite or adjacent coasts. Article 84 places the coastal States under the obligation to show on charts the outer limit lines of the continental shelf and the lines of delimitation drawn according to Article 83. Alternatively, where appropriate, those charts may be replaced by lists of geographical coordinates of points, along with relevant geodetic datum. Article 84 also requires coastal States to give due publicity to those lines or lists of coordinates. Coastal States must deposit a copy of these charts and lists with the Secretary-General of the United Nations and with the Secretary-General of the Authority in the case of the outer limit lines of the continental shelf. This is due to the fact that outer limit lines represent the maximum extent of the national jurisdiction, which also serves to define the Area (Article 134, paragraph 3, and Article 1, paragraph 1(1)).

2.2.4   Before analysing the implementation of the revenue sharing provisions under Article 82, it is first necessary to undertake a more detailed assessment of the resources over which coastal States hold sovereign rights of exploration and exploitation (see Article 77).

2.2.5   Article 82, paragraph 1, refers to 'non-living resources' in contrast with 'mineral resource' referred to in paragraph 3 of the same Article. The phrase 'non-living resources' incorporates more than merely 'mineral' resources, since mineral resources are also non-living resources, while not all non-living resources are 'mineral resources'.[11] In this respect, it is important to recall that in the context of Part VI, paragraph 4 of Article 77 provides sovereign rights over 'natural resources' which are defined as the mineral and other non-living resources of the seabed and subsoil, together with living organisms belonging to sedentary species that at the harvestable stage, either are immobile on or under seabed or are unable to move but in constant physical context with the seabed or the subsoil. The term 'mineral' is not defined here (or anywhere in the Convention) although such a definition is unlikely to be controversial (see Glossary for an example, and Annex 2). Other 'non-living resources' are also undefined, but examples such as sand, coral or aggregate rock could conceivably be included in this category. Section 4 of this paper provides some guidance to the potential significance and (in general terms) the value of a range of the most significant non-living mineral resources to be found in many parts of OCS areas, globally.

2.2.6   The inclusion of sedentary living organisms in Article 77 is the result of considerable discussion during UNCLOS III (Nandan et al., 1993). Paradoxically, living organisms – sedentary or otherwise – are not included in the scope of Article 82, and while they are beginning to attract interest as resources of great potential value, they are not discussed further in this report. Certain sedentary species of the deep ocean floor, however, are receiving substantial attention from the biomedical and pharmaceutical industries, as these animals often contain compounds used with success in, among other things, cancer treatment involving tumour shrinkage and statin development (UNEP, 2006). It is anticipated by some that the value of such resources of the continental shelf and deep ocean floor could support an industry worth billions of dollars a year. Their absence from the provisions of Article 82, therefore, despite their inclusion in Article 77, could well rob potential recipients of production revenue of a significant resource.

2.2.7   While of critical background importance to developing an understanding of the implementation of Article 82 in a coastal State's OCS, specific questions regarding: (a) the interpretation of Article 76 by coastal States; (b) its implementation by technical and legal groups in generating claims for submission to the CLCS; and (c) the process by which outer limits of the continental shelf are defined, are all matters that fall largely outside of the scope of this paper. The reader is referred to summary texts contained in Nordquist et al. (2004) and the recent reports of the International Law Association (ILA 2002, 2004, 2006 and 2008), among others, for recent overviews of these subject areas.

---

[11] It has been suggested that "the more generic and over-arching term of 'non-living' resources was utilized to include liquefied hydrocarbon resources, which might not otherwise have been considered to fall within the notion of solid 'mineral' resources," International Law Association, Rio de Janeiro Conference Report (2008).

3. PREDICTED RESULTS OF THE APPLICATION OF ARTICLE 76 ON A GLOBAL BASIS

3.1 The areas of continental shelf beyond 200M

3.1.1   In 1978, as part of the support work to the Third Conference on the Law of the Sea, a preliminary study (A/CONF.62/C.2/L.98) was made by the Secretariat illustrating various formulae for the definition of the continental shelf. The second addendum to the document included a chart showing the possible extent of continental shelf beyond 200M, to which was attached an explanatory document.[12] From this chart, an original estimate of 33 coastal States likely to establish their continental shelf beyond 200M began to emerge, but as discussed above, a more accurate figure, based on the updated information available in 2009, is more likely to be closer to 70. Many coastal States will make more than one submission, as they take advantage of the Rules of Procedure of the Commission allowing for partial or joint submissions. Expected submissions already exceed 90, excluding those to be made by coastal States for which the 10-year time limit has still not expired, and those coastal States with significant potential for continental shelf beyond 200M, that are not yet a State Party to the Convention, such as the United States of America.

3.1.2   In total, present submissions by coastal States for continental shelf beyond 200M cover in excess of 23 million square kilometres (sq km) of seafloor and subsoil. By comparison, it is estimated that the world's EEZs total some 85 million sq km, and the total area of the oceans beyond national jurisdiction – the Area, administered by the Authority in respect of mineral resources – covers approximately 260 million sq km. It is difficult to be definitive on these estimates, but as understanding improves of the way outer shelf areas are to be determined the figures will be steadily refined.

3.1.3   Of the 69 States estimated as having strong claims to continental shelf area beyond 200M, the majority are developing countries (see Table 2).

TABLE 2. LIST OF COASTAL STATES WITH POTENTIAL FOR CONTINENTAL SHELF AREAS BEYOND 200M

1	Liberia (25 September 2008)	8	Vanuatu (10 August 1999)
2	Congo (9 July 2008)	9	**Suriname (9 July 1998)**
3	Morocco (31 May 2007)	10	**Gabon (11 March 1998)**
4	Denmark (16 November 2004)	11	**South Africa (23 December 1997)**
5	Canada (7 November 2003)	12	**Portugal (3 November 1997)**
6	Madagascar (22 August 2001)	13	**Benin (16 October 1997)**
7	Bangladesh (27 July 2001)	14	**Chile (25 August 1997)**

---

[12]   A/CONF.62/C.2/L.98, with the initial calculation of areas affected as A/CONF.62/C.2/L.98/Add.2 and the third addendum included a letter from IOC-UNESCO as Add.3.

15	United Kingdom of Great Britain and Northern Ireland (25 July 1997)	43	Barbados (12 October 1993)
16	Equatorial Guinea (21 July 1997)	44	Uruguay (10 December 1992)
17	Solomon Islands (23 June 1997)	45	Seychelles (16 September 1991)
18	Mozambique (13 March 1997)	46	Micronesia (Federated States of) (29 April 1991)
19	Russian Federation (12 March 1997)	47	Angola (5 December 1990)
20	Pakistan (26 February 1997)	48	Somalia (24 July 1989)
21	Spain (15 January 1997)	49	Kenya (2 March 1989)
22	Papua New Guinea (14 January 1997)	50	Democratic Republic of the Congo (17 February 1989)
23	Malaysia (14 October 1996)	51	Brazil (22 December 1988)
24	Palau (30 September 1996)	52	Cape Verde (10 August 1987)
25	New Zealand (19 July 1996)	53	Yemen (21 July 1987)
26	Mauritania (17 July 1996)	54	Guinea-Bissau (25 August 1986)
27	Norway (24 June 1996)	55	Nigeria (14 August 1986)
28	Ireland (21 June 1996)	56	Trinidad and Tobago (25 April 1986)
29	Japan (20 June 1996)	57	Indonesia (3 February 1986)
30	China (7 June 1996)	58	United Republic of Tanzania (30 September 1985)
31	Myanmar (21 May 1996)	59	Guinea (6 September 1985)
32	France (11 April 1996)	60	Iceland (21 June 1985)
33	Republic of Korea (29 January 1996)	61	Togo (16 April 1985)
34	Argentina (1 December 1995)	62	Senegal (25 October 1984)
35	Tonga (2 August 1995)	63	Philippines (8 May 1984)
36	India (29 June 1995)	64	Côte d'Ivoire (26 March 1984)
37	Sierra Leone (12 December 1994)	65	Bahamas (29 July 1983)
38	Mauritius (4 November 1994)	66	Ghana (7 June 1983)
39	Australia (5 October 1994)	67	Namibia (18 April 1983)
40	Viet Nam (25 July 1994)	68	Mexico (18 March 1983)
41	Sri Lanka (19 July 1994)	69	Fiji (10 December 1982)
42	Guyana (16 November 1993)		

*   States listed in chronological order of their expression of consent to be bound by the Convention.

**   Entries in bold show States for which the Convention entered into force before 13 May 1999, and for which the date of commencement of the 10-year time period for making submissions to the Commission is 13 May 1999.

*** Other States shown (not in bold) are required to make a submission within 10 years of expression of consent date.

3.2 Continental shelf beyond 200 nautical miles in the polar regions

3.2.1   To complete this overview of areas covered by submissions to the CLCS and those that are expected over the next few years, this study has been extended to cover the polar areas of the Arctic Ocean and the waters around Antarctica. Compilations of the Arctic Ocean submissions are indicated in Figure 2, and include an estimate of the potential submission areas of other coastal States in the region (the Russian Federation and Norway have completed their cases, Canada and Greenland have until 2013 and 2014, respectively, to do so, and the USA has yet to ratify the Convention, giving it 10 years from the date of ratification to complete its case). The estimates of where the potential OCS for the three outstanding States will lie vary between authors (see for example, the alternative interpretations at http://www.nature.com/ngeo/journal/v2/n5/full/ngeo510.html), but it is likely that an area of between 650,000 and 750,000 sq km will constitute the combined OCS of the five relevant States, beyond which there will be two separate parts of the Arctic Ocean beyond national jurisdiction.

3.2.2   The Russian Federation case (see Figure 2) assumes that a sectoral principle prevails in constructing boundaries between neighbours in this region and has accordingly used the geographic North Pole as the northernmost point of its shelf area. Figure 2, however, also illustrates an alternative schematic solution to the boundary delimitation, based on constructing a line of equidistance between neighbouring areas. This simplified figure has been adapted from early syntheses by Ron Macnab.[13]

---

[13]   Pers. Comm.

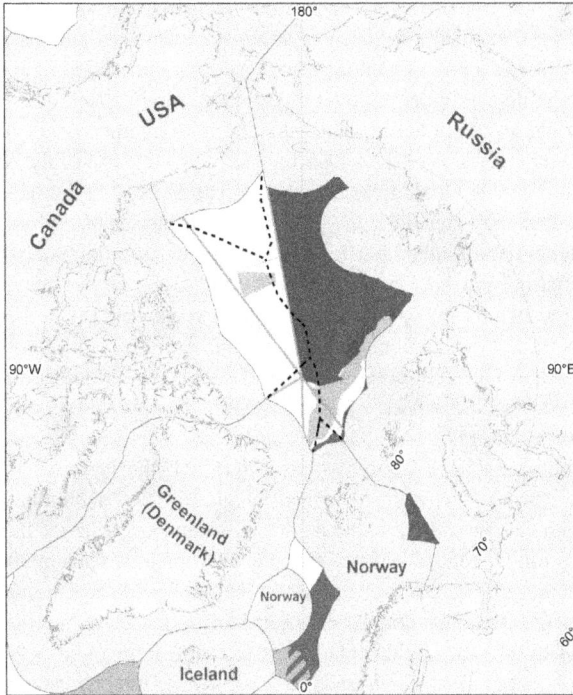

Figure 2. Stereographic polar projection of the Arctic Ocean region, illustrating area within 200M of baselines in pale blue, and beyond this, the areas currently submitted by coastal States in respect of continental shelf beyond the 200M limit. Purple - The Russian Federation (area constructed on sectoral principle, for discussion see text); Blue – Norway; Olive green – Iceland; Lime green – Denmark. Hatched colouring denotes where shelf areas overlap). Note that if boundaries were drafted on equidistant principles (see boundaries marked in dashed lines), potential areal coverage of each coastal State's OCS is as follows: USA -ca. 75,000 sq km; Denmark - ca. 45,000 sq km; Canada - >200,000 sq km.; Russia ca. 310,000 sq km. Grey areas denote possible areas beyond national jurisdiction – the Area. Green lines locate approximate boundaries where constructed on a sectoral basis (i.e., to meet at the geographic North Pole). This solution is favoured by Russia,[14] but apparently not by neighbouring States.[15] Further discussion on the likely maritime boundaries in the region beyond 200M is outside the scope of this report. A more recent, partial version of the construction in Figure 2 has been produced by the International Boundaries Research Unit, Durham, UK.[16] Chart provided by NOCS UNCLOS Group.[17]

---

[14] See http://www.un.org/Depts/los/clcs_new/submissions_files/submission_rus.htm.
[15] See http://www.un.org/Depts/los/clcs_new/submissions_files/rus01/CLCS_01_2001_LOS__ CANtext.pdf.
http://www.un.org/Depts/los/clcs_new/submissions_files/rus01/CLCS_01_2001_LOS__DNKtext. pdf http://www.un.org/Depts/los/clcs_new/submissions_files/rus01/CLCS_01_2001_ LOS__NORtext.pdf http://www.un.org/Depts/los/clcs_new/submissions_files/rus01/ CLCS_01_2001_LOS__USAtext.pdf.
[16] http://www.dur.ac.uk/resources/ibru/arctic.pdf.
[17] http://www.unclosuk.org/downloads/PMH_9June_3.pdf.

3.2.3   Of the five States bordering the Arctic Ocean, only Norway and the Russian Federation have so far presented submissions to the Commission in respect of the outer limits of their continental shelves. Most of the seafloor and subsoil of the Arctic Ocean should fall under national jurisdiction, but between two and four areas should be beyond any national jurisdiction. The final geometry will be determined following recommendations of the CLCS on each of the cases. A July 2008 fact sheet from the United States Geological Survey indicated that "[T]he extensive Arctic continental shelves may constitute the geographically largest unexplored prospective area for petroleum remaining on Earth," estimating that "approximately 84 per cent of the undiscovered oil and gas [in the area above the Arctic circle] occurs offshore."[18] According to recent studies, "most of the offshore areas with the highest probability for the discovery of hydrocarbons (oil and natural gas) are well within the national jurisdiction of Arctic Ocean littoral States and that the areas beyond 200M in the Arctic Ocean basin are not seen as having a high or even middling probability for the recovery of hydrocarbon resources."[19]

3.2.4   For completeness, submissions to the CLCS that have included continental shelf areas adjacent to Antarctica are illustrated in Figure 3. These submitting States include Argentina, Australia, Norway, and the UK. New Zealand has reserved its right to make a future submission in respect of the continental shelf of Antarctica by the deposit of a note verbale with the Secretary-General; Australia has asked the Commission to defer consideration of the area of continental shelf adjacent to Antarctica; the UK has submitted areas that are a natural prolongation of land masses that lie north of 60°S, beyond the area covered by the Antarctic Treaty; and Argentina has extended its continental shelf area from mainland across to the Antarctic shelf. It should be noted that in its recommendations to Australia in respect of its submissions in the region, the CLCS agreed with, and adopted recommendations regarding OCS areas extending south of 60°S where these areas were natural prolongations of land territories lying north of 60°S.[20]

---

[18] http://geology.com/usgs/arctic-oil-and-gas-report.shtml.
[19] Ted L. McDorman, The Continental Shelf beyond 200 miles: Law and Politics in the Arctic Ocean, in: The World Ocean in Globalization: Challenges for Marine Regions, 21-23 August 2008, Oslo.
[20] See http://www.un.org/Depts/los/clcs_new/submissions_files/aus04/aus_summary_of_recommendations.pdf.

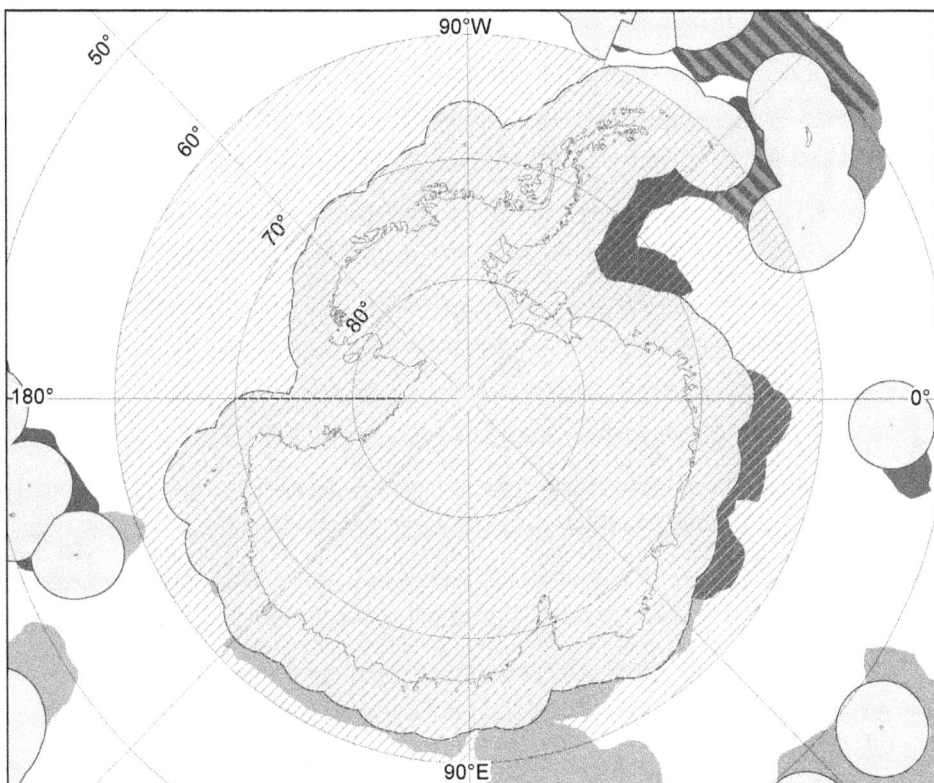

Figure 3. Stereographic polar projection of Antarctica, illustrating area within 200M of baselines in pale blue, and beyond this, the areas currently submitted by coastal States in respect of continental shelf beyond the 200M limit. Green – Australia submission;[21] Blue – Norway submission;[22] Orange – Joint submission between France and South Africa;[23] Purple – Argentina submission;[24] Red – UK submission;[25] (hatched where overlapping); Grey – New Zealand submission;[26] chart provided by NOCS UNCLOS Group.[27] Area south of 60°S[28] hatched in open grey lines.

---

[21] http://www.un.org/Depts/los/clcs_new/submissions_files/submission_aus.htm.

[22] http://www.un.org/Depts/los/clcs_new/submissions_files/submission_nor_30_2009.htm.

[23] http://www.un.org/Depts/los/clcs_new/submissions_files/submission_frazaf_34_2009.htm.

[24] http://www.un.org/Depts/los/clcs_new/submissions_files/submission_arg_25_2009.htm.

[25] http://www.un.org/Depts/los/clcs_new/submissions_files/submission_gbr_45_2009.htm.

[26] http://www.un.org/Depts/los/clcs_new/submissions_files/submission_nzl.htm.

[27] http://www.unclosuk.org/downloads/PMH_9June_3.pdf.

[28] http://www.ats.aq/e/ats.htm.

4. SUMMARY OF POTENTIAL RESOURCES IN THE OUTER CONTINENTAL SHELF

This section provides a general introduction to the most significant mineral resources identified in the marine environment, and informs discussion of the implementation of Article 82 by highlighting those that may have greater likelihood of occurrence on the OCS. Some comments are also offered regarding the likelihood of resource exploitation in the foreseeable future. The mineral resources described here are aggregates, placer deposits, phosphorite, evaporite deposits, polymetallic sulphides, polymetallic nodules and cobalt-rich ferromanganese crusts, hydrocarbons, and gas hydrates.

4.1 Aggregate

4.1.1   'Aggregate' refers to gravel, sand, clay, earth, shale, and stone, regardless of composition. This paper considers only offshore aggregate resources of sand and gravel as being of commercial interest.

4.1.2   Sand and gravel deposits are accumulations of rock fragments and mineral grains, derived from the weathering and erosion of hard rocks by glacial and fluvial action. Water action is an effective mechanism for wearing away weaker particles, and separating different sized fractions. The properties of sand and gravel largely depend on those of the rocks from which they were derived. Most sand and gravel is composed of particles that are durable and rich in silica (quartz, quartzite and flint), but other rock types, such as limestone, may also occur, and include negative impurities such as lignite, mudstone, chalk and coal.

4.1.3   Sand and gravel resources are unevenly distributed on the continental shelf but are similar to their land-based equivalents, occurring as small patches separated or covered by extensive areas of uneconomic deposits. They vary in their thickness, composition and grading, and in their proximity to the shore. They are often of high volume, but generally of low value.

4.1.4   Most extraction of aggregate takes place by dredging, and normally occurs in coastal waters less than 25 km offshore and in water depths of between 18m and 35m. Current dredging technology does not allow effective working in water depths in excess of 50m and it is therefore highly unlikely that such deposits would be significant beyond 200 nautical miles.

4.1.5   In summary, other than in exceptional circumstances, aggregates are not likely to be viable resources for exploitation in the OCS.

4.2 Placer deposits

4.2.1   Marine placer deposits are composed of detrital heavy metallic minerals that have become separated from their original settings or host rock-types that are comprised of lighter mineral associations, and which can commonly concentrate to form economically viable concentrations. The most economically important of these minerals are: cassiterite (tin); ilmenite (titanium); rutile (titanium); zircon (zirconium); chromite (chromium); monazite (thorium); magnetite (iron); gold and diamonds. While commonly recognised close to the points at which river or fluvial systems discharge into the sea, it is not easy to predict the occurrence of these deposits. The origin of some of the world's richest placer deposits, for instance, is closely related to Pleistocene glacio-eustatic changes of sea level, which resulted in the formation of two genetic types – fluviatile and beach deposits. Examples of both types occur off Namibia, although placer deposits are equally common off many coastal States (see International Seabed Authority (2001)).

4.2.2   Some of the most abundant fluviatile placer deposits are gold and cassiterite (tin oxide). They can accumulate on the inner shelf during glacial periods associated with falling sea level, where rejuvenated fluviatile erosion concentrates these heavy minerals in lag sediments. These can be further transported and concentrated on the shallow continental shelf during periods of falling sea level occurring during interglacial-to-glacial transitions, moving significant deposits some distance offshore in the process.

4.2.3   Beach placer deposits originate during periods of stable or slightly fluctuating sea level that are typical during intermediate glacial periods. Most were subject to dispersion or shoreward removal during periods of rising sea level during interglacial periods. The wealth of placer deposits along present shorelines is largely a result of transgressive beach-barrier migration, by which much of the shelf sand with its pre-concentrated heavy-mineral assemblages is moved to its present coastal position. This lateral and vertical migration was especially effective during the last two transitions from glacial to interglacial periods.

4.2.4   In summary, there is some possibility of placer deposits migrating beyond 200M where highly productive discharge sites, involving high-value minerals, wide shelf regions and episodes of low sea level stands, combine to transport minerals to OCS areas, although it would be quite exceptional for this to have happened widely. The South West African/Namibian shelf is the most widely recognised site where both widespread dispersal of the deposits and extant exploitation infrastructure is already in place, at least for shallow water operations.

4.3 Phosphorite deposits

4.3.1   World sub-sea resources of phosphorite are probably at least of the order of hundreds of billions of tonnes. Nonetheless, because of the prevailing downbeat economic conditions and the availability of phosphates from plentiful non-marine sources, no offshore mining is currently occurring or foreseen in the immediate future. Land deposits of phosphorite are large enough to meet world demands for the short and medium term, but sub-sea production may become economically viable in some local areas, especially those far removed from onshore deposits.

4.3.2   Offshore phosphorite deposits are precipitated in abundance adjacent to wide-margin coastal States affected by upwelling and displacement of deepwater current flow to shallower ocean levels. Principal sites would include the southern hemisphere margins of South America and Africa, and parts of Australasia and many of the western Pacific Island groups. In most cases, however, the deposits are either wholly within coastal States' EEZs, or some distance from shore and consequently of diminished economic interest, particularly with regard to the revenue sharing potential of Article 82.

4.3.3   In summary, phosphorite is not considered a likely mineral resource to be considered in the implementation of Article 82 provisions in areas of the continental shelf beyond 200M.

4.4 Evaporite deposits

4.4.1   Anhydrite and gypsum (calcium sulphates), common salt (sodium chloride), and associated potash-bearing minerals are collectively described as 'evaporite deposits'. They are formed by the evaporation of seawater and other natural brines in geologic basins of restricted circulation. Important deposits of magnesium-bearing salts are also deposited in such basins. Elemental sulphur forms in some basins by biogenic processes involving the alteration of anhydrite. In this direct sense, these minerals form an abundant, but low value resource. However, the particular physical properties of salt mean that it is of interest because of its association with hydrocarbons, especially oil.

4.4.2   Rock salt tends to flow at relatively low temperature and pressure, so salt in thick beds can be squeezed by the weight of a few thousand metres of overlying sediment, and often penetrates the overburden, protruding upwards to form salt domes, plugs and other structures. Such masses, which may easily be several kilometres in diameter, may bring salt to or near the surface. They also often form structures in the intruded sedimentary layers that may be favourable for the accumulation of petroleum, and the limestone cap rock associated with some of these masses may be the site of sulphur deposits.

4.4.3   Evaporites, including some potash and magnesium minerals and elemental sulphur, can be recovered by the Frasch process, which involves solution-mining methods that involve injecting hot water into reservoirs. Thus the presence of geothermal water sources near evaporite deposits greatly enhances their potential value.

4.4.4   Like phosphorite, land-based deposits of evaporites are so abundant and widespread that it is almost inconceivable that deep water marine deposits could become economical to extract, other than in exceptional economic or geographical circumstances.

4.4.5   In summary, evaporates are unlikely to feature in the evaluation of mineral resources of the OCS in connection to the implementation of Article 82.

4.5 Polymetallic sulphides

4.5.1   In the submarine environment, polymetallic sulphides form as remarkably pure and concentrated deposits along active spreading centres, or plate boundaries, where superheated bottom water first leaches minerals from newly formed ocean crust, then redeposits them at hydrothermal vent sites. These sites inevitably move away from the formation site as the tectonic plates migrate away from the spreading centre, carrying the deposits with them into the deep ocean on either side.

4.5.2   The majority of submarine polymetallic sulphides are massive ore bodies containing both high-temperature (ca. 350°C, or above) and low-temperature (<300°C) mineral assemblages. In varying proportions these comprise compounds – usually sulphides – of copper, iron, zinc in major amounts (such as pyrrhotite, pyrite/marcasite, sphalerite/wurtzite, chalcopyrite, bornite, isocubanite), barite, anhydrite, and amorphous silica, often with anhydrite (calcium sulphate). Some massive polymetallic sulphides at back-arc spreading centres also contain galena (lead sulphide), arsenic and antimony (in sulphosalts), and occasionally native gold. Other minor sulphides of tin, cadmium, antimony and mercury also commonly occur in varying amounts at different localities.

4.5.3   Polymetallic mineral deposits on the seafloor are intimately related to the formation of new oceanic crust by seafloor spreading. At mid-ocean ridges, convection-driven circulation of seawater through the oceanic crust is the principal ore-forming process. Seawater that penetrates into young oceanic crust is converted into hydrothermal fluid with low pH, low Eh,[29] and high temperature during wall-rock/ water interaction. It is generally thought that this process requires magmatic heat sources, such as the presence of a high level magma chamber, to drive the convection.

4.5.4   Hydrothermal fluid leaches and transports metals and other elements from their host rock to the surface of the seafloor. As they discharge, at temperatures up to 350°C from the 'black smoker' chimneys (and at water depths frequently in excess of 2,500m), the hydrothermal fluids mix with ambient seawater at temperatures ranging between 2°C and 5°C causing the continuous precipitation of metal sulphides at the seafloor (as mounds and chimneys) or as subsurface stock-works. The resulting sulphide deposits can reach considerable size. For example, the TAG hydrothermal mound (at the Mid-Atlantic Ridge [MAR] at 26°) is approximately 200m in diameter and around 50m high (Rona et al., 1993). Lower temperature 'white smoker' chimney systems are also present and generate minerals of considerable economic potential. In the southern Lau Basin, for example, the first examples of actively forming, visible primary gold in seafloor sulphides were documented at lower temperature hydrothermal sites.

4.5.5   Current exploration programmes for polymetallic sulphides within 200M of coastal States (such as the Solwara offshore sites in the Papua New Guinea EEZ) are reaching the extraction/exploitation phase in the active hydrothermal system of the Bismarck Sea (see Nautilus Minerals information at http://www.nautilusminerals. com). The world's first seafloor copper/gold mine is planned for the region in 1,600m of water and within 50 kilometres of land, but there is potential to move into deeper water and further offshore as systems are tested and economic conditions allow.

4.5.6   In summary, there is no doubt that polymetallic sulphides represent one of the more promising mineral resources common to the deep sea floor, and likely to occur within some OCS areas. Certain coastal States that are geographically associated with actively spreading mid-ocean ridge systems (such as Iceland and or the Portuguese Azores Islands Group) and that are able to sustain an argument for the natural prolongation of their continental margins (and continental shelves) along the mid-ocean ridge beyond 200M are highly likely to have polymetallic deposits of some kind in these areas. Recent analyses of vent distributions in the North Atlantic suggest that one high temperature vent site per 100km of active slow-spreading ridge is an acceptable, but perhaps conservative, approximation.[30]

---

[29] Eh, or reduction potential, is a common parameter used by marine researchers in hydrothermal exploration. Tracking Eh in water column chemistry is a means to detect and characterise vent systems and their discharge.

[30] Pers. Comm., G. Cherkashov, March 2010.

4.6 Polymetallic manganese nodules and cobalt-rich ferromanganese crusts

4.6.1   Manganese nodules are micro- to potato-sized concentrations of iron and manganese oxides that can contain economically valuable concentrations of nickel, copper and cobalt (up to about 3 per cent, combined). They occur mainly on the deep sea floor, but have been reported throughout many of the ocean's physiographic provinces. Apart from manganese and iron oxide, nickel, copper and cobalt, the nodules can include trace amounts of molybdenum, platinum and other metals.

4.6.2   Manganese nodules were first dredged during the HMS *Challenger* expedition to the Pacific Ocean in 1872-76. The current knowledge of manganese nodule and crust distribution is based on large amounts of information from sidescan sonar, drill cores, dredged samples, seafloor photographs, video records and direct observation from submersibles. This reveals that, while nodules occur in deep water throughout all major ocean basins, the highest abundance and most attractive grades are found in two areas. These are the Eastern Central Pacific Ocean between the Clarion and Clipperton Fracture Zones, [31] and the Indian Ocean.

4.6.3   Cobalt-rich ferromanganese crusts, similar in composition to the nodules, are found in some areas as coatings or encrustations on hard rock substances, on seamounts and the submerged portions of islands. They range in thickness from a few millimetres to layered crusts several centimetres thick. As much as 25 cm of crust has been reported on a number of occasions. The material is deposited on sand grains, pebbles, rock fragments and outcropping bedrock, or may blanket unconsolidated sediments and can contain up to 2 per cent in cobalt.

4.6.4   Manganese nodules and cobalt-rich manganese crusts are likely to be the most commonly occurring mineral resource in a coastal State's OCS. These deposits may be the most significant for coastal States in low latitudes, and due to their widespread occurrence, it is unlikely that configuration of the (geological) shelf moderates their distribution.

4.6.5   In summary, there is little doubt that manganese nodules and cobalt-rich crusts will occur in many coastal States OCS areas. Their relatively low value, but high local abundance and grade, make these deposits a likely candidate for consideration under a system for the implementation of the provisions of Article 82.

4.7 Hydrocarbons

4.7.1   Oil and natural gas are hydrocarbon deposits that occur naturally within thick sedimentary sequences. These are largely confined to the continental shelves, continental slopes, continental rises and small ocean basins. Hydrocarbons provide the major energy source for modern civilisation, delivering power for heating, lighting, telecommunications, industrial and agricultural machines, and all forms of transport. Hydrocarbons also form the raw material for numerous products ranging from plastics to fertilisers.

---

[31] For most recent source of reference material, see the results of the Workshop on the Establishment of a Geological Model of Polymetallic Nodule Resources in the Clarion-Clipperton Fracture Zone (CCZ) of the Equatorial North Pacific Ocean: http://www.isa.org.jm/files/documents/EN/Pubs/2003-GeoModel.pdf.

4.7.2   Hydrocarbons are mainly formed in marine sedimentary basins. These geologic environments contain strata comprising mineral and biochemical elements including, importantly, unoxidised organic matter. Over millions of years, the sequence is buried further during subsequent sedimentation, and becomes subjected to high pressures and temperatures. These conditions fractionate the organic material, forming liquid (oil) and gaseous (natural gas) hydrocarbons. Oil may comprise between 50 and 90 per cent hydrocarbons, with oxygen, nitrogen and sulphur in minor quantities.

4.7.3   Generally, large quantities of hydrocarbons can only be formed in settings where appropriate source materials are available, and at depths normally greater than around 3,000m of sediment overburden. The formation of exploitable reservoirs of hydrocarbons requires migration (from its source rocks) to geological traps comprised of a porous reservoir rock overlain by an impermeable horizon (or a 'cap-rock'). Common geological traps for hydrocarbons include: shales; salt domes (evaporites); and anticlinal folds of permeable and non-permeable rock layers. Ideal environments for hydrocarbon formation and retention may be provided by sedimentary sequences in excess of 1,000m thickness, in areas of high-heat flow, and comprising organic-rich layers at depth overlain by porous rocks that are in turn overlain by impermeable, domed strata.

4.7.4   In addition to liquid hydrocarbons, natural gas is commonly formed in association with crude oil. However, because of its lower viscosity, gas may often be found apart from oil reservoirs.

4.7.5   There is little doubt that conventional hydrocarbons, both oil and gas, are the main focus of attention in terms of well documented resources on 'wide' continental margins with OCS potential. Largely due to the reluctance of oil companies and exploration companies to invest heavily in areas 200M beyond coastal States beyond of uncertainties regarding sovereignty (in potentially disputed areas) or the absence of any licensing administration, these areas have seen little new surveying or sampling in recent years. The lack of data with which to evaluate frontier area capacity has severely hindered progress towards understanding the distribution and value of these deep water resources. However, there is an expectation that, once claims have been submitted under Article 76, areas of OCS will attract increased attention and exploration investment, and that their suitability for prospecting and resource potential will become better understood.

4.7.6   In summary, hydrocarbons represent the most mature and well understood mineral resources likely to occur in OCS areas. Technologies exist or are in hand to deal with deposits in the 'ultra' deep water that dominates the OCS, and the market is always hungry for new sources. It would seem natural to establish the basic principles of the implementation of Article 82 using conventional hydrocarbons as a model, but one that allows adaptation to embrace other resources, as discussed above.

4.8 Gas hydrates

4.8.1   Gas hydrates are solid, ice-like compound substances formed of cubic crystalline lattices of water and gas. They occur worldwide as layers or laminar units interbedded with sediments in the upper few hundred metres of core samples of drill sections taken on continental margins. They are formed by the natural process of organic decay in marine sediments, under a range of pressures (greater than 500m water depth) and temperatures (dependant on depth) that make the gas hydrate molecule stable. Methane is the main component of the gas, often present in excess of 99 per cent (Kvenvolden, 1993). When the host water is in its solid state (ice), its open molecular structure encages gas molecules with great efficiency, securing methane by up to 170 times the volume of the ice itself. This gas is released when the ice melts, but this is not considered to be the greatest of the properties of hydrate; much more interesting is the fact that the ice layer can act as an impermeable cap, or 'seal' to hòld in gaseous methane in huge volumes. As the technology delivering effective extraction of gas from beneath gas hydrate caps is still very much in its infancy, the resource potential of gas hydrates, while real, awaits investment and development.

4.8.2   Gas hydrates occur abundantly, both in Arctic regions (at or just below the seafloor) or at depth in marine sediments elsewhere. They look very much like water ice. Methane hydrate is stable in ocean floor sediments at water depths greater than 300m below the sea floor, where it is known to cement loose material in a layer several hundred metres thick.

4.8.3   Gas hydrates form and accumulate where marine sediments contain suitable and sufficient dissolved gas and where the geothermal (subsurface temperature gradient) conditions are within the stability field of the hydrate. The source of the dissolved gas is the breakdown of organic matter trapped within the sediment. Therefore, the unoxidsed organic carbon content of the sediment is a significant factor in determining the potential for gas generation.

4.8.4   The methane hydrate pressure (depth) - temperature stability field shows that these conditions may be met at water depths greater than about 300-500m on the continental slope (dependant on bottom water temperature), reaching some depth beneath the deep sea floor (determined by the geothermal gradient). The introduction of higher molecular-weight gases (ethane or propane) to the methane allows hydrate gas mixture to form at lower pressures and therefore to be stable in shallower water or at higher temperature. However, the presence of salts in pore water shifts the gas hydrate phase boundary and decreases the gas hydrate stability area, requiring deeper and/or colder conditions for formation and accumulation.

4.8.5   Gas hydrate reservoirs of methane are identified as a potential future natural resource, possibly comprising up to ten times the fuel value of current conventional gas and oil resources (Collett, 1992; Gornirz and Fung, 1994). Thus, the distribution of gas hydrate deposits is of growing strategic importance.

4.8.6   In summary, gas hydrate is probably the widest distributed, yet so far least accessible mineral resource of the OCS. Technologies under development in Japan, India and the USA are all seeking to establish a working industry scale extraction system that is both cost effective and safe, but it is still a long way from being delivered.

5. SUMMARY OF CURRENT METAL MARKET AND OIL AND GAS TRENDS AND PREDICTIONS

5.1   We now turn to global trends and developments in supply, demand and prices for minerals of primary interest to the deep-sea mining industry. Some comments are made on the current status of world resources and reserves for four of these principal products – cobalt, copper, nickel and manganese. Additional comments reflect the current volatility of the markets and commodity pricing. Market prices naturally fluctuate, and although some longer term trends can be used as indicators of the potential value of marine resources, absolute pricing on any individual metal should be made according to a particular date and recorded exchange rate.

5.2   The post-2002 upswing in global economy activity has been the strongest for 30 years. Global gross domestic product rose by 21 per cent between 2003 and 2007, and the volume of world trade increased by about 39 per cent over the same period. All regions shared to varying degrees in this growth, with China and other Asian countries in the lead. Their growth is strongly biased towards materials intensive investment.

5.3   Over time, technological improvements and changes in the structure of demand have more than offset the declining ore grades and reserve depletion of most minerals. The trend of real prices has therefore been stable or declining, but with strong cyclical variability. Costs also move cyclically, with the mining industry's costs largely moving with other industries' prices. There is complex feedback between prices and costs and the latter are not independent of prices. Investment in new capacity is driven by expectations of future prices, and these are heavily influenced by recent experience. Average prices realised over a period are usually very different from the prices ostensibly required to justify new investment, and they are normally much lower. Prices invariably overshoot their equilibrium levels, both in recessions and in boom periods. Although production costs provide a floor to prices, there is no ceiling.

5.4   The recent global economic downturn, however, is likely to see a significant reduction in demand for many metals. For example, aluminium demand has already been heavily reduced due to massive cuts in car production. Consumers are also not investing in expensive items using stainless steel, such as refrigerators and washing machines, and this has seriously hit nickel markets.

5.5   About 90 per cent of the manganese ore produced globally is used in the iron and steel industry. With global output of steel growing slowly, the use and production of manganese ore has trended downwards, with cyclical fluctuations. However, if increase in demand remains at the current rate it would suggest that demand for manganese will expand from 11.5-12 million tonnes of contained manganese in 2007, to 17-18 million tonnes by 2015, thus causing demand for ore on a gross weight basis to rise to some 50 million tonnes.

5.6   About two thirds of the output of primary nickel is used in stainless steel production. The balance goes into a range of uses including non-ferrous and ferrous alloys, electroplating, batteries and chemicals. There is a marked volatility in the market, partly linked to the availability of nickel containing scrap. Global demand has been increasingly biased towards China, which accounts for over a quarter of the demand. Nickel markets have been hit particularly hard by the current global economic downturn.

Large onshore nickel producers have been cutting production as reduced metal prices make operations uneconomical.

5.7   Cobalt has developed a new lease of life over the past decade, with demand and production rising by nearly 11 per cent per annum. Its traditional uses have been supplemented by growth in the markets for catalysts and rechargeable batteries. Moreover, cobalt's use in super alloys has been boosted by a surge in aircraft production. Output in newly mined cobalt has recently flattened out and fallen short of demand because the Democratic Republic of the Congo (DRC), the biggest mine producer, imposed controls on exports of unprocessed cobalt in 2006 in order to encourage greater development of downstream processing in the country.[32]

5.8   Reductions in cobalt demand, particularly from China in late 2008, however, led to the suspension of some mining operations in the DRC in early 2009. With prices currently at a two-year low, poor prospects for cobalt mining may be offset by the continued phenomenal demand for raw materials from China and Asia. In addition, mining companies are facing additional financial constraints as many companies have lost up to 90 per cent of their share prices. Reduced consumer demand for electrical goods has resulted in a fall in cobalt demand for batteries, but the demand in aerospace manufacturing appears robust and likely to continue. Despite the reduced prices given the global financial uncertainty and recessionary pressures new projects are anticipated to be finalised during 2010, the Cobalt Development Institute expects a volatile price period in the medium term, and a softening over the periods of further strengthening in the developing Eastern markets.[33]

5.9   Global usage of copper grew by an average of 3.5 per cent between 1992 and 2007, although contrary to many perceptions, the average growth rate has been lower than in previous years (3.3 per cent between 2001 and 2007). As with nickel, growth has been led by China and the Asian countries. The International Copper Study Group, an intergovernmental organization that promotes international discussion and cooperation on issues related to copper, forecasts small surpluses during 2008-2009, with output rising faster than demand in the following years.

5.10   Global copper prices have also been hit by the economic downturn, although they have not suffered as much as those for other metals. Copper inventories were until recently in deficit, which underpinned high prices. Prices have fallen by nearly 60 per cent from a record high of about US$3,200 per tonne in July 2008, and as a result global production has decreased. Analysts predict that copper will recover faster from the global economic downturn than many other metals.

5.11   The location of mining is continuously changing as reserves are depleted and new mines are developed. Only continued successful exploration and development can ensure that a company or country can meet its existing share of rising global demands. This demand will fluctuate cyclically in the future, just as in the past, around a rising trend. New mine capacity is always needed, not only to fulfil that demand, but also to compensate for the considerable depletion of existing mines. Today, some 70,000-90,000 tonnes of new nickel mine capacity are required annually, as well as 0.8 million tonnes of copper, 5,000 tonnes of cobalt, and 1.5-2 million tonnes of manganese ore,

---

[32] http://www.thecdi.com/cdi/images/documents/facts/cobalt_facts-supply_demand_07_.pdf.
[33] http://www.thecdi.com/.

on a gross tonnage basis. These requirements will grow with rising demand. Deep-sea mining will not substitute for land-based material but contribute to the world's rising needs alongside new land-based development.

5.12   Capital Analysts Inc., a business to business brokerage firm,[34] predicted little, if any, growth in global consumption for most metals during the first half of 2009, with a growing risk that global demand may reduce. Market surpluses are leading to reduced costs, and although production cuts are being increasingly introduced to counter this, the market outlook for many metals appeared bleak going into 2009. Analysts predicted that copper prices will be amongst the first to recover, but that the near-term nickel price outlook was poor, largely due to a significant downturn in stainless steel demand. As predicted, global supply did exceed demand in most metal markets between January and November 2009, although exceptions included nickel and lead.

5.13   Current cuts in established onshore metal ore mining suggest a poor near-term outlook for deep-sea mining. Large mines, such as Anglo-American's Loma nickel mine in Venezuela, have temporarily halted production (as of January 2009) as reduced metal prices make operations uneconomical. The uncertainties and increased costs of deep-sea mining make this sector look particularly vulnerable to fluctuations in global economic conditions. This is evidenced by recent press releases from Nautilus Minerals Inc., one of the most successful and enterprising marine mineral exploration and processing companies. Following recent announcements that it would be 'slowing' its plans for mining deep water polymetallic sulphides until further notice, it has this year reported the discovery of a number of high-grade sulphide systems, with good assay results, establishing a platform for an intensive drilling campaign in the Western Bismarck Sea during 2010.[35]

5.14   A direct analysis can be secured by comparing land and sub-sea mining prospects and deposits. Identified world cobalt resources amount to about 15 million tonnes. The vast majority of these resources are in nickel-bearing laterite deposits, with most of the rest occurring in nickel-copper sulphide deposits hosted in mafic and ultramafic rocks in Australia, Canada and the Russian Federation, and in the sedimentary copper deposits of DRC and Zambia. While the metal market recognizes that millions of tonnes of hypothetical and speculative cobalt resources exist in manganese nodules and crusts on the ocean floor, there is a reluctance to rely on these as a viable source in the near future. Similarly, a recent assessment of the USA's copper resources indicated 550 million tonnes of copper in identified (260 million tonnes) and undiscovered (290 million tonnes) resources. A preliminary assessment indicates that global land-based resources exceed 3 billion tonnes. Meanwhile, a (highly speculative) estimate of deep-sea manganese nodule resources includes about 700 million tonnes of copper.

5.15   Identified land-based resources averaging 1 per cent nickel or greater would yield at least 130 million tonnes of the metal, with about 60 per cent in laterites and 40 per cent in sulphide deposits. The extensive deep-sea resources of nickel found in the manganese crusts and nodules covering large areas of the ocean floor, particularly in the Pacific Ocean, may be of some interest to an industry keen to supply the nickel-based battery and superalloy markets, and other niche products.

---

[34] www.capitalanalysts.com.
[35] http://www.nautilusminerals.com/s/Media-NewsReleases.asp?ReportID=380619&_Type=News-Releases&_Title=Nautilus-Minerals-Discovers-Five-High-Grade-Copper-Zinc-Systems.

5.16   Projections for oil and gas demand over the next two decades were recently summarized in *International Energy Outlook 2009*, published by the Energy Information Administration.[36] World energy consumption is set to grow by 44 per cent between the period 2006 and 2030, mostly in the nations outside the Organisation for Economic Cooperation and Development (OECD). With barrel prices for oil as high as US$147 in July 2008, and as low as US$34 in early 2009, it is hard to predict how much of a constraint cost will be, but clearly any access to new sources of supply would have a positive effect on the market, and so areas in the OCS will become more important in securing stable supplies of oil and gas. The current worldwide economic downturn, however, is dampening world demand for energy in the near term, as manufacturing and consumer demand for goods and services slows. In the longer term, with economic recovery anticipated after 2010, most nations will return to trend growth in income and energy demand.

5.17   Oil and gas together make up by far the largest component of the world's energy supply, and although new sources such as biofuels, ethanol and coal/coke-derived products are significant, liquid hydrocarbons are likely to retain this status. It seems inevitable that demand in the transport sector is likely to rise faster than in any other, driven largely by growth in rapidly modernizing developing countries, despite the global concerns about carbon emissions and climate change (EIA, 2008). Sources of oil and gas beyond current frontiers of 200M from territorial sea baselines will be carefully watched as the trend of the barrel price approaches a projected US$200 in 2030 (EIA, 2008).

---

[36] www.eia.doe.gov

6. NON-LIVING MINERAL RESOURCES: CURRENT EXPLORATION AND EXPLOITATION TECHNIQUES

This section provides a brief overview of the status of the exploitation of mineral resources in the deep ocean. Many 'recently recognised' non-living resources remain at the frontier of extraction technology, where infrastructure requires considerable and lengthy investment and development. Others, such as oil and gas, enjoy mature industries, some of which are already becoming active and effective in the deepest water depths at continental margins.

6.1 Conventional oil and gas hydrocarbons

6.1.1   Exploration and exploitation technology for oil and gas deposits is well developed and, due to sustained demand, is continually being developed to address more 'frontier' areas and conditions. The deepest water production stands at more than 3,050m (in the Gulf of Mexico). As operators approach the 200M EEZ limit, problems stemming from distance from land-based infrastructure are routinely overcome. There has been little change to the idea that oil and gas deposits occurring in exploitable water depths beyond 200M will be readily recovered.

6.1.2   Current offshore operations continue to break new ground and set records in technological achievement. A new discovery, known as the Tiber field, was made 250 miles southeast of Houston and is being developed using the very large *Deepwater Horizon* rig. The platform dangled about a million pounds of well casing while floating in 1,260m of water, and then drilled another 9,425m below the sea floor. Temperatures at the sea floor were about 35 degrees, while the temperature of fluids in the well miles below was 250 degrees. The exploration well used to find the Tiber field was the deepest vertical well ever drilled.

6.1.3   The massive *Perdido Spar* rig is another record beater, becoming as of 2010 the deepest operating offshore rig working in water depths of more than 2,400m. The wells drilled will be in excess of 3,000m according to the operator, Shell. With oil prices now flirting with $100 a barrel, this type of ultra deep water exploration, which will be required in the OCS in even greater depths of water, is not far off the horizon.

6.2 Gas hydrates

6.2.1   Gas hydrate research has taken off rapidly over the past 5-10 years, following a long period of inactivity that reflected larger oil companies' vested interest in conventional hydrocarbons. India, the USA, the UK and especially Japan (not least at the Canadian-Japanese partnership in the Mackenzie Delta deposit)[37] have devoted considerable resources into both academic and applied commercial research to assess the feasibility of extraction of natural gas from hydrate or from areas of trapped gas. Much interest now focuses on gas hydrate as a resource, with developed commercial-scale extraction potential within 10-20 years.

---

[37]   http://aapgbull.geoscienceworld.org/cgi/content/abstract/86/11/1971.

6.2.2   Significant safety and environmental concerns, however, are also associated with the presence of natural gas hydrates, ranging from their possible impact on the safety of conventional drilling operations to the influence on Earth's climate of periodic natural releases into the atmosphere of large volumes of hydrate-sourced methane or derivative carbon dioxide. Considerable research is needed to characterize more completely and accurately the location, composition, and geology of Earth's natural gas hydrate deposits. This body of research is a necessary precursor to the development of means to extract them, as well as to determination of their possible future climatic impact.

6.3 Polymetallic sulphides

6.3.1   Polymetallic sulphides are recognised on land as a readily accessed focussed mineral source, generally occurring at shallow levels. In the marine environment, they have been assessed by particulate mapping as a by-product of scientific research at active sites. Some interest is developing in shallow seismic and potential field (magneto-telluric, resistivity, electro-magnetic, deep-tow magnetic and gravity) techniques, or a combination of both. The geology/geochemistry-based search for techniques to identify gossans - weathered, inactive sites where active hydrothermalism has ceased and the deposition of metallic ores has concluded - should also be highlighted, as interest is growing in possibilities of mining recently inactive sites where extraction difficulties presented by extreme temperatures and caustic fluid flow are minimised.

6.4 Polymetallic nodules and cobalt-rich ferromanganese crusts

6.4.1   Technology related to the exploration and exploitation of other mineral resources with some economic potential for exploitation (manganese nodules and cobalt-rich ferromanganese crusts) is in various stages of development. Pilot extraction instrumentation has been trialed by a number of investors with respect to manganese nodule mining (notably, several of the current contractors with the International Seabed Authority for exploration blocks in the Eastern Pacific Ocean). Less well advanced are effective, large-scale strategies for the extraction of cobalt crust deposits, although with the impending establishment of regulations by the Authority for these deposits, this situation is expected to change in the near future.

6.4.2   Crust distributions on seamounts are complex and controlled by many factors such as seamount morphology, current patterns, mass wasting, substrate rock type and age, subsidence history. Development of this potential resource ultimately depends on crust distribution, as well as small-scale topography, grade, and tonnage. The parameters that will be used to define a mine site are becoming clearer as more research is carried out, but data collected over the past 25 years can be used to bracket permissive characteristics.[38] One of the greatest impediments to progress to extraction is the economics of raw metal price and the significant investment that will be needed to migrate extant test collector rigs to full scale mining platforms.

---

[38]   http://www.cprm.gov.br/33IGC/1317067.html.

7. EXAMPLES OF CURRENT LICENSING REGIMES FOR HYDROCARBONS

This section summarises the legislation covering oil and gas exploration by three countries – the United Kingdom, Canada and Norway – and provides a background to the possible development of a licensing regime for areas of OCS to which Article 82 may apply.

Although these are examples of mature governance systems, this very maturity may mean that they are harder to modify to meet Article 82 provisions. By contrast, some developing States with new hydrocarbon industries would be required to develop licence regimes from relative infancy, unencumbered by an established system.

7.1 The United Kingdom

7.1.1   In the United Kingdom, the Petroleum Act 1998 vests all rights to the nation's petroleum resources in the Crown. But the Secretary of State for Energy and Climate Change can grant licences that confer exclusive rights to "search and bore for and get" petroleum. Each of these licences confers such rights over a limited area and for a limited period. The Secretary of State has discretion in the granting of licences, which he exercises to ensure maximum exploitation of this valuable national resource, but there are other considerations that he must also take into account, for example, protection of the environment and the interests of other users of the sea.

7.1.2   Licences can be held by a single company or by several working together, but in legal terms there is only ever a single Licensee, regardless of the number of companies involved. All companies on a Licence share joint and several liability for operations conducted under it. Each Licence takes the form of a Deed, which binds the Licensee to obey the licence conditions regardless of whether or not it is in use.

7.1.3   Offshore licensing began with the North Sea boom of the 1960s. The United Kingdom Government's Licensing system covers oil and gas within Great Britain, its territorial sea and the United Kingdom Continental Shelf. Northern Ireland's offshore waters are subject to the same licensing system as the rest of the United Kingdom Continental Shelf. The Isle of Man issues Licences for its own onshore area and territorial waters.

7.1.4   Each Licence carries an annual charge, called a 'rental'. They are charged at an escalating rate on each sq km that the Licence covers at that date. Rentals have two purposes: they encourage Licensees to surrender acreage they do not want to exploit, to free it up for others who do; and they concentrate Licensees' minds on the acreage they actually decide to keep.

7.1.5   Seaward Production Licences and Petroleum Exploration and Development Licences are valid for a sequence of periods, called 'Terms'. These Terms are designed to follow the typical lifecycle of a field: exploration; appraisal; and production. Each Licence expires automatically at the end of each Term, unless the Licensee has made sufficient progress to earn the chance to move into the next Term.

7.1.6   The Initial Term is usually an exploration period. For Seaward Production Licences, this is normally set at four years, although it can be longer for 'frontier'

Licences. For Petroleum Exploration and Development Licences, this is set at six years. The Initial Term carries a Work Programme of exploration activity that the United Kingdom Government and the Licensee agree during the application process. The Licence expires at the end of the Initial Term unless the Licensee has completed the Work Programme by then. At that time the Licensee must also relinquish a fixed amount of acreage (usually 50 per cent), which is another due diligence requirement designed to ensure that the Licensee has explored the whole acreage over the period of the Initial Term.

7.1.7   The Second Term is intended for appraisal and development, and lasts four years for Seaward Production Licences and five years for Petroleum Exploration and Development Licences. The Licence expires at the end of the Second Term unless the Secretary of State approves a Development Plan by then. Assuming the Development Plan has been approved and enacted within the Second Term, the licence moves forward into the Third Term, involving production.

7.1.8   The Third Term is intended for production, and lasts 18 years for Seaward Production Licences and 20 years for Petroleum Exploration and Development Licences. The Secretary of State has the discretion to extend it if production is continuing, but the UK Government reserves the right to reconsider the provisions of the Licence before doing so, especially the relevant acreage and rentals.

7.2 Canada

7.2.1   Oil and gas activities off Canada are governed by four principal Acts:

- The Canadian Petroleum Resources Act (CPRA) governs the lease of federally owned oil and gas rights on "frontier lands" to companies wishing to explore for and produce hydrocarbons. "Frontier lands" include the territorial sea and the continental shelf.
- The Canada Oil and Gas Operations Act (COGOA) governs the exploration, production, processing and transportation of oil and gas in marine areas controlled by the federal government (the territorial sea and continental shelf). Areas controlled by the provincial government are not included.
- The Canada-Newfoundland Atlantic Accord Implementation Act and the Canada-Nova Scotia Offshore Petroleum Resources Accord Implementation Act, otherwise known as the 'Accord Acts', implement agreements between the federal and provincial governments relating to offshore petroleum resources.

7.2.2   Calls for bids from oil companies in respect of blocks made available for specific licencing rounds are published at least 120 days before the closing date for submission. A call for bids will specify the frontier lands to which the interest is to apply, and any other terms and conditions that the bid must satisfy.

7.2.3   An exploration licence confers the right to explore for, and the exclusive right to drill and test for petroleum; the exclusive right to develop the relevant frontier lands in order to produce petroleum; and the exclusive right to obtain a production licence. The standard term for an exploration licence is nine years. However, if the drilling of any well has commenced prior to the term of the exploration licence, it may continue in force while the drilling of the well is being pursued diligently, and for so long thereafter as necessary to determine the existence of a significant discovery based on the results of that well.

7.2.4   On the expiration of an exploration licence, any related frontier lands and that are not subject to a production licence or a significant discovery licence become Crown reserve lands.

7.2.5   Where a significant discovery has been made, the National Energy Board will make a 'declaration of significant discovery'. Following this a significant discovery licence may be issued by the Ministry responsible for Energy, Mines and/or Petroleum Resources in that province, which allows for the rights to exploration, drilling and testing for petroleum, the exclusive right to develop the licence area for petroleum production, and the exclusive right to obtain a production licence.

7.2.6   At any time after the declaration of significant interest, the appropriate Ministry may issue a Drilling Order requiring the owner of the interest to drill a well on any portion of the significant discovery. Drilling must commence within a year of the Order being made, or within a longer period if specified by the Minister within the Order.

7.2.7   The production of petroleum, and title to the petroleum produced, follows the issue of a Production Licence. A Production Licence is effective from the date of issue and for a term of 25 years. If petroleum is being produced commercially on the expiration of a Production Licence, the term is extended while commercial production continues. A Production Licence, or share in a Production Licence, may only be held by corporations incorporated in Canada.

7.2.8   On expiration of a Production Licence, the related frontier lands become Crown reserve lands.

7.3 Norway

7.3.1   Petroleum licensing off Norway is controlled by the Ministry of Petroleum and Energy (MPE), with input from the Norwegian Petroleum Directorate (NPD), by the issue of production licences. Production licences are issued via two different schemes: ordinary licence rounds (usually biannually); and Awards in Predefined Areas (APA awards), which are issued annually. The APA scheme relates to mature areas on the continental shelf, and is intended to encourage exploration near areas of existing infrastructure.

7.3.2   An ordinary licensing round starts when the MPE invites oil companies to nominate blocks that they believe should be included in the announcement. MPE and the NPD perform a thorough review of the proposed blocks, which involves consultation with fishery and environmental authorities, before announcing the blocks for which a company can apply for a production licence. Environmental and/or fishery conditions may apply to an individual block. Companies can apply individually or as part of a group.

7.3.3   Prior to application for a production licence, new companies must meet pre-qualification criteria. The Norwegian Petroleum Act stipulates that companies must establish an organisation in Norway with competence in resource management, health, safety and the environment. Required technical competence must also be demonstrated.

7.3.4   The MPE awards production licences based on the applications received. When awarding licences the authorities consider a company's technical expertise, understanding of geology, financial strength and experience.

7.3.5   The production licence provides exclusive rights to carry out surveys, exploration drilling and production of oil and gas within a defined geographical area. The licence is valid for an initial (exploration) period of between four and six years. The licensees can apply to extend this period up to 10 years. During this period, a specific work commitment must be completed, seismic acquisition or exploration drilling.

7.3.6   If the exploration phase proves successful, the company may apply for an extension to the production licence, typically for up to 30 years. If exploration does not prove the presence of oil or gas, the area can be relinquished at the end of the initial period. For licences awarded before 2004, the company can demand to keep up to one half of the area of the production licence for 30 years.

7.3.7   Norway's twentieth ordinary licensing round closed for bids on 7 November 2008. The round covered areas on the Norwegian continental shelf in the Norwegian Sea and Barents Sea. A new scheme was invoked for this licensing round involving a broad-based public consultation as to which blocks should be included in the round. The aim of this was to promote more transparency in the licensing process, and to ensure critical examination of the social and technical consequences of proposed exploration and production. Norway initiated its twenty-first licensing round on 5 November 2009, and bids are currently in preparation for the next blocks on the Norwegian continental shelf.

8. DISTRIBUTION OF OFFSHORE RESOURCES IN RELATION TO AREAS OF DIFFERENT REGULATORY REGIMES

8.1   Uncertainties related to resources that straddle maritime boundaries may arise, involving areas of the seafloor under different jurisdictions, or areas subjected to exploration and exploitation programmes established by different coastal States. In order to illustrate some of these differences, and the potential difficulties in accommodating the way mineral resource exploitation could be undertaken, a theoretical distribution of marine mineral resources and territorial delimitation has been made for two adjacent coastal States (Figure 4). The example contains coastline, agreed land and maritime boundaries, the 200M EEZ and an outer limit of continental shelf as defined by Article 76. In addition, three areas of proven mineral resource deposits (here assumed to be hydrocarbons of conventional oil and/or gas composition) are distributed in a series of discrete areas, or fields. The figure exaggerates the consequences of a particular spatial relationship with areas of maritime space defined according to international law (in this case, LOSC). The scenario has been constructed to illustrate the potentially different jurisdictions of two coastal States, and the location of these areas (and resources) in relation to seabed areas beyond national jurisdiction, where the Authority is responsible for the development of mineral resources. A number of issues deriving from this geometry of maritime boundaries and associated juridical responsibilities are discussed below.

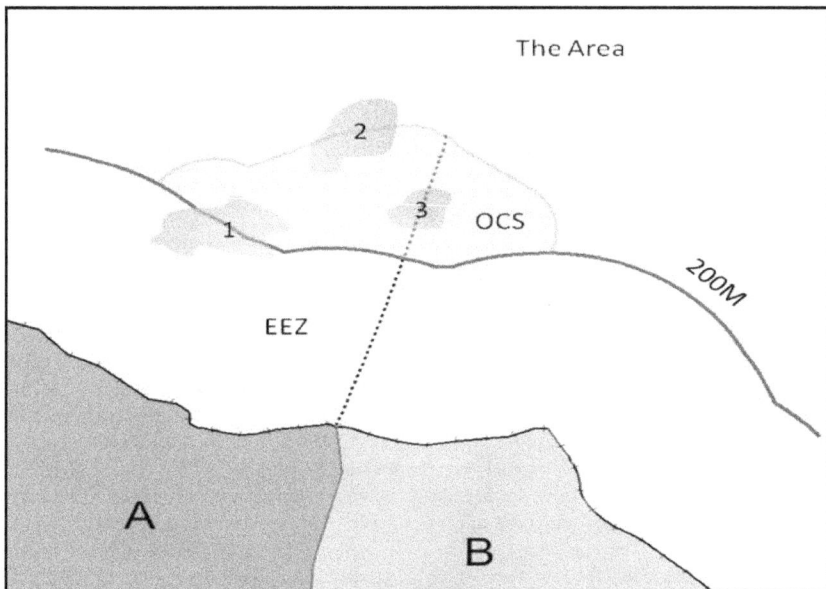

Figure 4. Theoretical scenario relating to maritime space within and beyond national jurisdiction, entitlement to resources by coastal States and the Area.

Figure 4 illustrates the land areas of two coastal States, A and B, and their potential offshore maritime territories. The theoretical maritime jurisdictional areas are indicated as follows: the red line delimits the EEZ; the orange line delimits the outer limits to the continental shelf area or the region; the dotted line is equidistant between the offshore areas of States A and B. Three oilfields are indicated as polygons marked 1, 2 and 3, each of which straddles one of the types of maritime boundary illustrated in this model.

8.2   States A and B both have offshore resource potential represented by the oil fields numbered 1, 2 and 3, but their access to these sites varies depending on the location of the deposit relevant to their boundaries with each other, and with the Area. Neighbouring States strategies with respect to exploitation of the deposits may be constrained by different licensing regimes. State A has access to some part or proportion of all three oil fields, but State B has only partial access to oil field 3, which lies beyond the 200M limit of its EEZ, and which is subject to the relevant articles and provisions contained in Part VI of the Convention. In normal practice, where reservoirs are cut by a jurisdictional boundary, agreements are reached between the parties to proceed under some sort of shared production, such as unitisation, or a similar joint development agreement.[39] We will follow this procedure in our example.

8.3   In Figure 4, oil field 1 transects the 200M EEZ boundary of State A, and naturally State A has full rights to the exploitation of oil in the sector within its EEZ. Beyond this boundary, however, while State A enjoys the sovereign rights to oil exploration, production in the field could potentially be required to proceed under a different licensing and operational regime. Areas beyond 200M would be subject to the additional revenue-sharing requirements under the implementation of Article 82. In an extreme case, where production has been in operation under a licensing system inside 200M for a significant period, a potentially less attractive licensing system taking into account the provisions of Article 82 may subsequently be imposed on the oceanward part of oil field 1. Careful monitoring of extraction on each side of the maritime boundary would be necessary to ascertain that appropriate apportionment of production (and revenue through Article 82) was ensured, and that a variant of the "rule of capture"[40] was not invoked to justify extraction only within the EEZ, with inevitable impact on the envisaged revenue sharing under Article 82.

8.4   Further complications could arise during the development of a production strategy for oil field 2. In this case, a single operator accesses the resource underlying

[39] Kendall Freeman (2007). Oil and gas deposits at international boundaries, http://www.eapdlaw. com/files/News/beea97f3-7544-42e1-be4d-00e1e25f9d2a/Presentation/NewsAttachment/bf4112ae-d66c-4209-a623-06c8f8a3214c/Oil%20and%20gas%20deposits%20at%20international%20 boundaries%20-%20March%202007%20-%20Kendall%20Freeman%20Guidance%20Note.pdf.

[40] The 'rule of capture' or 'law of capture' is common law from England, adopted by a number of United States jurisdictions, that determines ownership of captured natural resources including groundwater, oil, gas and game animals. The general rule is that the first person to 'capture' such a resource owns that resource. For example, a landowner who extracts or 'captures' groundwater, oil or gas from a well that bottoms within the subsurface of his land acquires absolute ownership of the substance, even if it is drained from the subsurface of another's land. A corollary of this rule is that a person who drills for groundwater, oil or gas may not extract the substance from a well that bottoms within the subsurface estate of another by drilling on a slant.

the OCS of coastal State A, and is subject to the appropriate revenue payment regime derived from the implementation of Article 82. It is likely that a different licensing regime would relate to the part of the resource lying beyond the outer continental shelf (i.e., in the Area); one that is not subject to the same revenue sharing provisions in Article 82. A single operator for the field would need to reconcile the different methods of operation for each part of the deposit. As above, vigilant and independent monitoring would be needed to negate concerns of extraction under the rule of capture.

8.5   It might also be useful to speculate on the level of development of these theoretical neighbouring States. Let us suppose that State A is a developed State, while State B is a developing state, and unlike its neighbour, is a net importer of oil and gas. State B will not be obliged to supply payments of any kind to the Authority, and could in theory operate a more favourable licensing regime than A. Alternatively, State B may consider that it is in its best interests to keep the resource unexploited, as an investment for the future, while State A has an urgent need to extract. How could this be resolved? Would this juxtaposition of different obligations and legal constraints moderate the way the field was exploited, or (if applicable) the terms under which a joint system of development was negotiated and agreed? An additional consideration is that a time differential may well exist between the two States' ratification dates; State B may lag behind in the Article 76 process and have ratified several years later than State A. Its submission to the CLCS regarding its OCS may be still in development. State B may have elected to apply the advice provided in SPLOS/183, thereby delaying its submission still further. All of these eventualities will impact on State A's ability to develop an equitable exploration and exploitation regime.

8.6   There are technical considerations in respect of the assessment, and auditing of payments as part of Article 82 revenue, which are offset by recovered costs (resources used in connection with the exploitation), as laid out in paragraph 2 of Article 82. It will be necessary to secure accurate and verifiable information regarding value or production volume at a site to ensure the derivation of appropriate income from the revenue sharing process, as demonstrated in the theoretical examples discussed above. Volume would appear in principal a relatively easy parameter for which to supply records, and the supply of such information to the Authority under some form of confidentiality arrangement seems straightforward. Verification of these figures, however, would seem to be an exercise requiring significant expertise and funding well outside the remit, or indeed mandate, of the Authority. Conversion of the volume into the value of the production, if that was to be the preferred deliverable of the State, would also seem straightforward, but in a fluctuating economic context where oil (and other mineral resource) prices are subject to rapid and dramatic variation, the timing and method of any calculation of revenue (on an annual or aggregated monthly basis?) becomes critical. Again, this is an issue that needs more monitoring and administrative resources.

8.7   It remains to be seen how willing an oil producer might be to provide such critical information in the situation described above, especially if maintaining a competitive edge meant restriction, rather than dissemination of that information. It would be completely understandable if producers find it difficult to provide the consistent information the Authority might require to calculate and verify revenue amounts.

8.8   Equally important, but perhaps less difficult to monitor would be the verification of the status of the State as a net importer of the mineral resource under exploitation. It is assumed that accurate and auditable country statistics of this kind could be secured from the appropriate ministry of the State concerned.

8.9   Many of the considerations referred to in this section have implications for the Authority's administration and overview of the implementation of the provisions of Article 82. As far as can be seen, no funds have been identified to support what will inevitably be a major task of data collection, and the checking and verification of States' production in the outer continental shelf. Retrieving information, and collating and maintaining a secure database with which to calibrate the process of collection of revenue, will place a severe demand on the Authority's resources. With scores of States potentially requiring such monitoring, the workload of the technical operators of this scheme will be significant, and inevitably, costly. On the other hand, outsourcing such an operation would require considerable funding and potentially unpopular reallocation of States Parties' contributions.

9. SOME CASE STUDIES OF POTENTIAL CLAIMS TO CONTINENTAL SHELF AREAS BEYOND 200 NAUTICAL MILES

In this section, a number of coastal States with potential continental shelf areas beyond 200M are discussed in terms of their likely resource bases and exploration programmes. The examples include States with margins characterised by wide, sediment-rich shelves, complex platform margins and elevated ridge-like features.

9.1 Brazil

9.1.1   On 17 May 2004, Brazil became the second coastal State to make a submission to the CLCS. Its continental margin includes the Amazon Fan, one of the world's largest single sedimentary deposits, along with many sediment-rich basinal areas within and beyond 200M, some of which already host mature petroleum extraction operations. When looking at conventional hydrocarbon resources, Brazil's deepwater margin has a high proven resource capacity, and benefits from the geological setting of a deepwater fan and margin with significant potential for gas hydrate deposits. Furthermore, Brazil is one of the world leaders in the development of ultra-deepwater hydrocarbon exploration and production technology. Brazil therefore has current capacity and long-term potential to exploit both conventional and future hydrocarbon resources.

9.1.2   Other resources within the outer continental shelf, however, are far less well quantified, although geological conditions are such that none of those discussed in section 4 can be excluded as potential resources. In fact, Brazil may be the first State to receive a request for a licence to recover a mineral resource from an area beyond 200M (see footnote 4, above). In 2008, a mining consortium applied to extract coral-based aggregate material from the OCS between the mainland and the Islands of Trindade and Martin Vaz. At the time of writing, the Brazilian government is considering the appropriate mode of licensing.

9.1.3   In terms of other resource potential, however, the picture is less promising. The robust supply of sediment, which is a feature of much of the continental margin, would tend to inhibit nodule or crust growth. Upwelling is not a significant feature of the continental margin, so phosphorites are not widely documented. It is possible, however, to make some preliminary estimates of the parts of the OCS that may have the greatest potential for conventional oil and gas deposits, based on their geological setting. Figures 5 and 6 illustrate the key features of the margin's deepwater geology that are relevant to the oil industry. As a guide, a sediment thickness of more than 3,000m can be considered the minimum overburden that could provide the necessary pressure and temperature conditions to 'cook' the organic source matter and generate oil and gas – a system commonly referred to as the 'kitchen'. Naturally, on their own, these conditions are insufficient to guarantee hydrocarbon production; they are only part of the several essential elements of a successful hydrocarbon system. Other critical factors required are: a suitable source rock to provide the organic material; a reservoir rock of appropriate porosity to contain the hydrocarbons once formed; and an impermeable seal, or cap rock, formation to prevent the leakage and escape of oil and gas.

9.1.4   This arbitrary guide based on thickness of sedimentary overburden is used here to give a generalised indication of potential resource, but as in all cases discussed below, is only indicative. To enhance understanding of how accessible any potential oil and gas resource might be within the OCS area, those parts of the continental margin lying in less than 3,000m water depth have been highlighted in Figures 5 and 6. This value is a useful current benchmark water depth at which exploration/exploitation of hydrocarbons is currently readily carried out, although technology is pushing this limit steadily into deeper.

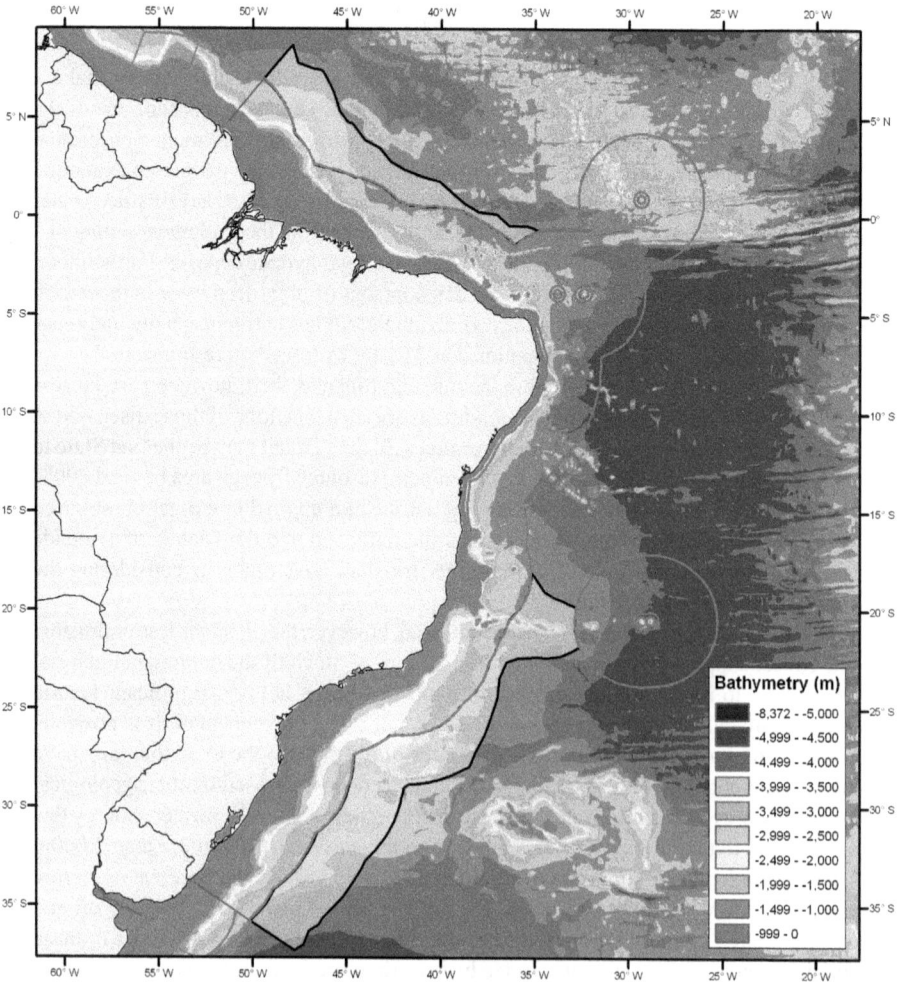

Figure 5. The submitted outer limits of the Brazilian continental shelf shown by pale shaded area beyond 200M limits in red (final limits subject to CLCS recommendations, source www. un.org/Depts/los/clcs_new/submissions_files/submission_bra.htm).

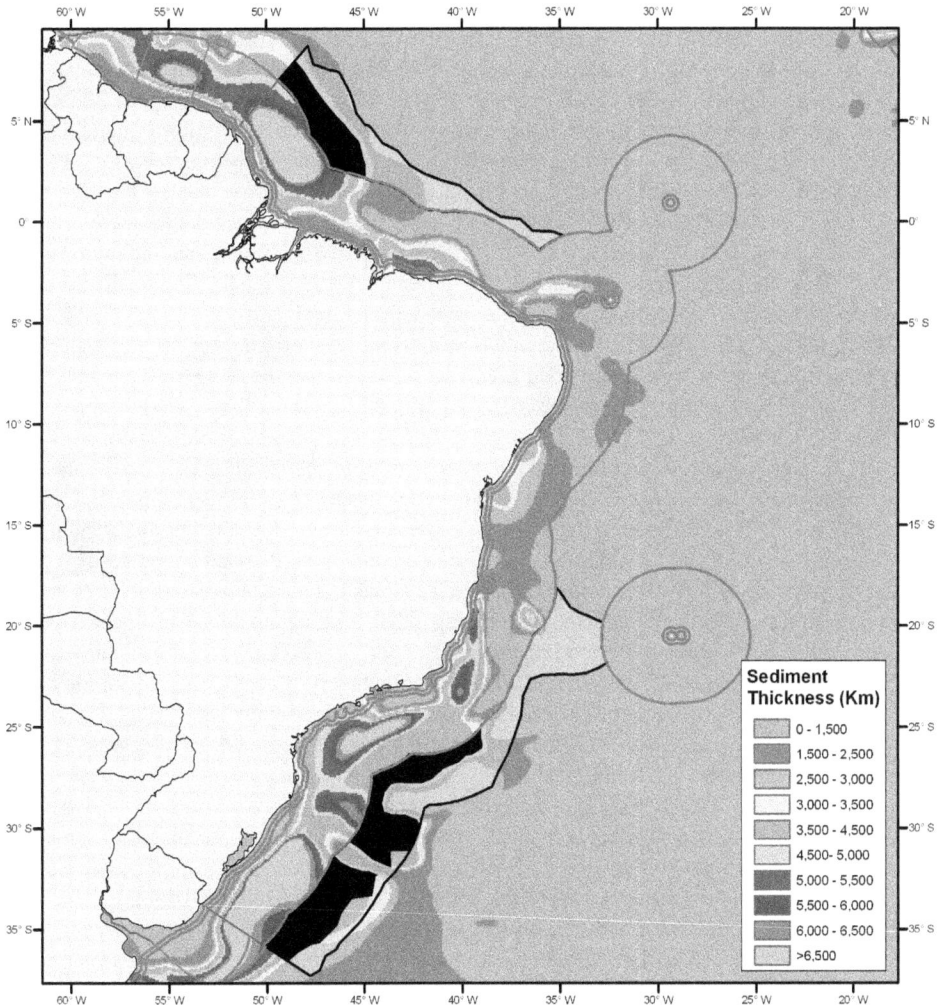

Figure 6. The Brazilian OCS area, illustrating sediment thickness and OCS submission limits. Sediment thickness along the margin in excess of 3,000m is identified from National Geophysical Data Center (NGDC) modelled distribution (source www.ngdc.noaa.gov/mgg/ sedthick/sedthick.html). Black areas show the thick sediment section in water depths of 3,000m or less, which are the areas considered as having highest petroleum potential and accessibility parameters.

9.1.5   Brazil has experienced rapidly expanding oil, natural gas, and electricity consumption in recent years. It has the second largest crude oil reserves in South America, and is one of the fastest growing oil producers in the world. Natural gas constitutes only a small portion of Brazil's total energy consumption, and it has the third largest electricity sector in the Western Hemisphere.

9.1.6   In 2004, Brazil submitted to the CLCS an area of OCS totalling 925,925 sq km, which was split between 332,590 sq km in a northern area and 593,335 sq km in the southern area. Recommendations regarding the outer limits of the continental shelf were adopted by the CLCS on 4 November 2007. Brazil has yet to take these recommendations, which differ significantly from their submission into its national maritime legislation. Nevertheless, the entire area, and its non-living mineral resources will be subject to the provisions of Article 82.

9.1.7   With sediment thickness in excess of 5km in water depths between 2,000m and 4,500m, Brazil has a very real potential of hydrocarbon exploitation in its OCS. Over the past 23 years, Petrobras, forerunner in the use of the floating production concept, has emphasized innovation and upgrade based on its professional expertise. The first initiative – PROCAP, a technological development programme for deepwater production systems – was launched in 1986 in order to improve the company's technical skills in oil and natural gas production in water depths up to 1,000m. To accomplish this, the Albacora and Marlin fields were chosen as a development unit. The results obtained by this first programme and other discoveries in deeper water encouraged the company to create a new programme, and in 1993, PROCAP-2000 was launched.

9.1.8   As in the rest of the world's deepwater margin States, the oil industry in Brazil is expanding and developing a set of new technologies, boosted by the desire to begin production in both its already discovered deepwater fields, and potential fields in water depths of around 3,000m. Estimates using rather crude parameters of prospectivity and current accessibility described earlier in this report suggest that more than a third of the Brazilian continental shelf beyond 200M offers, in theory, potential and accessibility for hydrocarbon exploitation. These areas exist in water depths that vary from 2,000m to 4,500m. However, only 55,500 sq km of the sediment-rich OCS exist at a water depth of 3,000m or less, further restricting the likelihood of early exploitation.

9.1.9   Ultimately, resources of likely economic significance for Brazil may include gas hydrate. This deposit is likely to occur in many parts of the continental margin, and several deep seismic surveys have revealed indirect indicators, although these await verification. Manganese nodules also exist, but according to academic analyses, they have proven to date to be scarce and of relatively uninteresting composition. In common with rifted and sedimented margin in general, the potential for polymetallic sulphides as a viable deposit is unlikely to be great, but there is potential near the hotspot-derived volcanic Trindade and Martin Vaz Islands, and at off-ridge axis locations adjacent to the St Peter and Paul Island Group in the central Atlantic. Finally, cobalt-rich ferromanganese crusts are unlikely to occur in economically feasible amounts, also due to the high sedimentation rate that militates against widespread optimum conditions for nucleation on bare rock surface accumulations. Crust deposits in the Atlantic Ocean are generally hugely inferior and economically unviable in comparison with those in the Pacific Ocean.

9.2 Angola

9.2.1   Angola has one of the most attractive continental margins in terms of well-recognised, ultra deep-water hydrocarbons, both documented and predicted, close to its 200M limit. These deposits are made up of conventional oil and gas, and gas hydrate. The existing mature hydrocarbon infrastructure available to Angola could mean a relatively rapid migration to a full-scale extraction and access programme once the CLCS has made its recommendations regarding the limits to the continental shelf beyond 200M. Angola's preparation for its submission to the CLCS is well developed, and it provided its indicative and preliminary information regarding the outer limits of its continental shelf on 12 May 2009.

9.2.2   The estimated area of continental shelf beyond 200M to be targeted by Angola is yet to be determined (Figure 7). Its submitted indicative material suggests a wide OCS, extending perhaps as far as 350M from its territorial sea baselines.[41] This figure takes no account of the potential overlap of neighbouring coastal States' submissions at its northern limits.

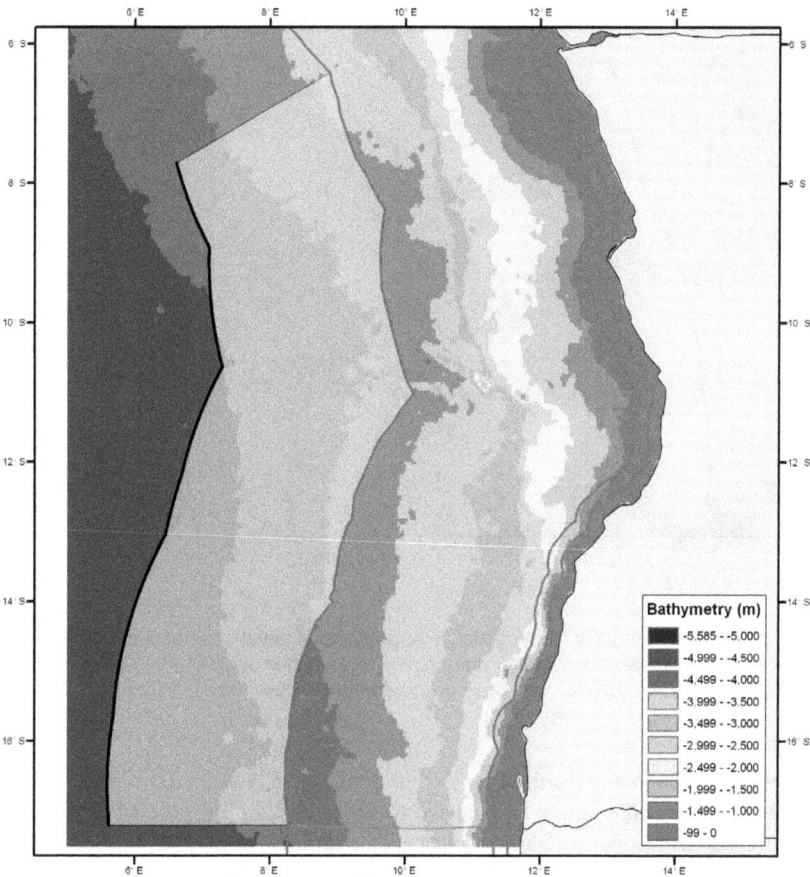

Figure 7. Predicted bathymetry off Angola. Key: 200M limit in red; 350M limit in black; possible OCS area shaded. Note that water depths for almost the entire potential OCS exceed 3,500m.

[41] http://www.un.org/Depts/los/clcs_new/submissions_files/preliminary/ago2009preliminaryinformation.pdf.

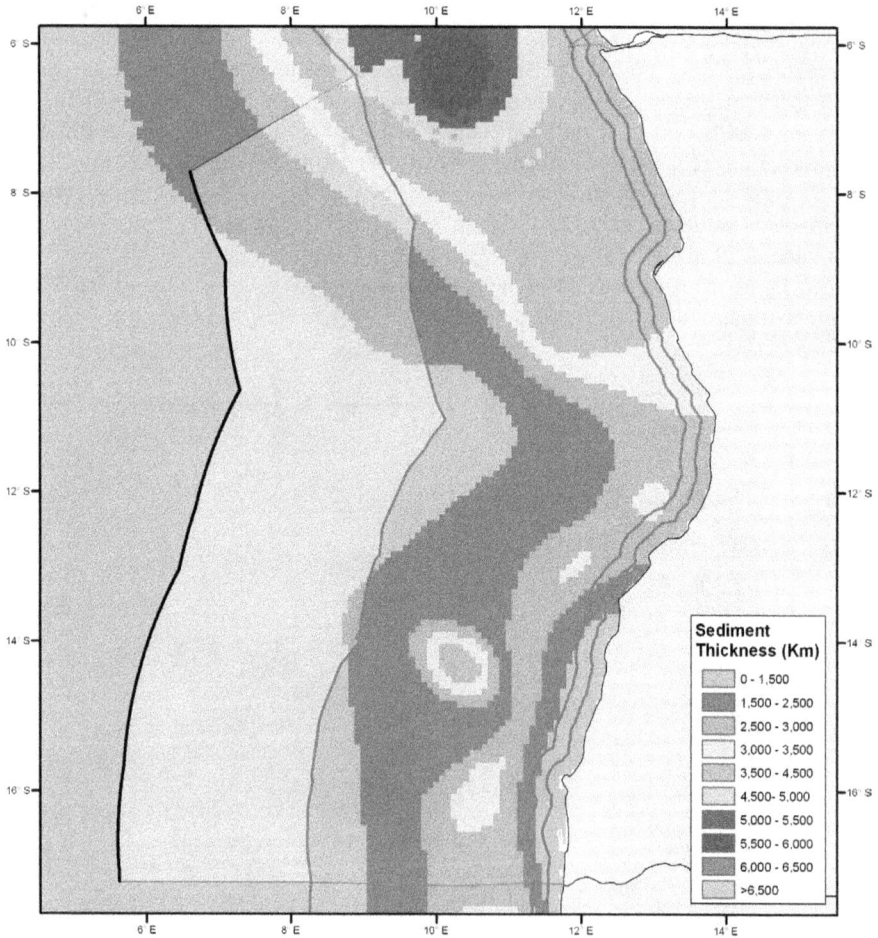

Figure 8. Highest potential for prospective Angolan continental shelf beyond 200M. These areas lie in the northern continental margin, where modelled sediment thickness is greater than 3,000m (source: NGDC www.ngdc.noaa.gov/mgg/sedthick/sedthick.html).

9.2.3   Angola is the third largest oil producer in Africa after Nigeria and the Libyan Arab Jamahiriya and is expected to see significant oil production increases in the short-term as new offshore projects come online. On January 1, 2007, Angola became the twelfth member of the Organization of the Petroleum Exporting Countries (OPEC), and in December of that year, received an oil production quota of 1.9 million barrels per day (bbl/d), effective from January 1, 2008.

9.2.4   Angola, however, is still rebuilding the infrastructure destroyed during the country's 27-year civil war that came to an end in 2002. Although the country is beginning to see growth and stability, challenges persist: around 70 per cent of the population still lives on less than US$1/day; the World Bank ranks Angola as one of the most difficult places in the world in which to do business as a result of corruption and bureaucracy; and there are persistent allegations of lack of transparency in public finance.

9.2.5   In recent years, China has agreed to provide multi-billion dollar oil-backed loans to fund infrastructure development. These loans are costly and repayment depends heavily on international oil prices. However, Chinese support has placed Angola in a position from which it could break ties with the International Monetary Fund (IMF) over economic support programmes that require, among other things, governance and transparency. Nonetheless, the country is experiencing high levels of foreign direct investment, particularly in the oil sector.

9.2.6   Academic research in the region shows that this continental margin (like many sub-Saharan West African continental margins) is characterized by common occurrences of gas hydrate deposits.[42] None are included in current exploration programmes because technology has yet to overcome the problems associated with extraction, but indirect indicators show that the deposits are prevalent in the deepest waters of the EEZ, and by implication they also exist extensively in the continental shelf beyond 200M.

9.2.7   There seems little chance of high abundance and high-grade examples of other non-living mineral resources in the Angolan continental shelf beyond 200M, although nodules and crusts are always a possibility. Once again, the high sediment supply that increases the potential of hydrocarbon-based resources is likely to suppress (or at the least, conceal) other types of deposit.

9.3 Canada

9.3.1   Canada provides a good example of a very wide margin coastal State with a continental shelf already featuring intense exploitation of oil and gas at a range of water depths. Mature operations are under way across the EEZ, out to and beyond the 200M limit, and high prospectivity is a characteristic of the shelf areas throughout.

9.3.2   Canada has two areas where potential continental shelf beyond 200M is likely to be exploited – in the north-west Atlantic Ocean and in the Arctic Ocean. The total area of continental shelf beyond 200M covers approximately 1.3 million sq km, although the exact figure may be much higher. Canada has until 7 December 2013 to make its submission in respect of its OCS to the CLCS.

9.3.3   Approximately 781,700 sq km of Canada's continental shelf beyond 200M lies off its Atlantic margin. Figure 9 illustrates this coverage, and for reference, includes the location of the Hibernia oil field, in 80m water depth, which is currently producing hydrocarbons within 37M of the 200M limit. Not only is the site a prime example of exploration at distance from land, but it also represents success in combatting an extremely inhospitable environment characterized by rogue waves, fog, icebergs and sea ice, hurricanes and winter storms.

---

[42] For example, Charlou et al., *Chemical Geology*, Volume 205, Issues 3-4, 14 May 2004, pp. 405-425.

9.3.4   Since operations started, in November 1997, the Hibernia field has proven to be the most prolific oil well in Canada, with initial production rates in excess of 50,000 BOE[43] per day from a single well. A dedicated fleet of shuttle tankers continuously operates between the platform and an onshore storage terminal adjacent to an oil refinery at Come By Chance. Hibernia demonstrates that, providing the right economic climate prevails, operational difficulties and infrastructure challenges relevant to the development of the continental shelf beyond 200M, however severe, are generally surmountable.

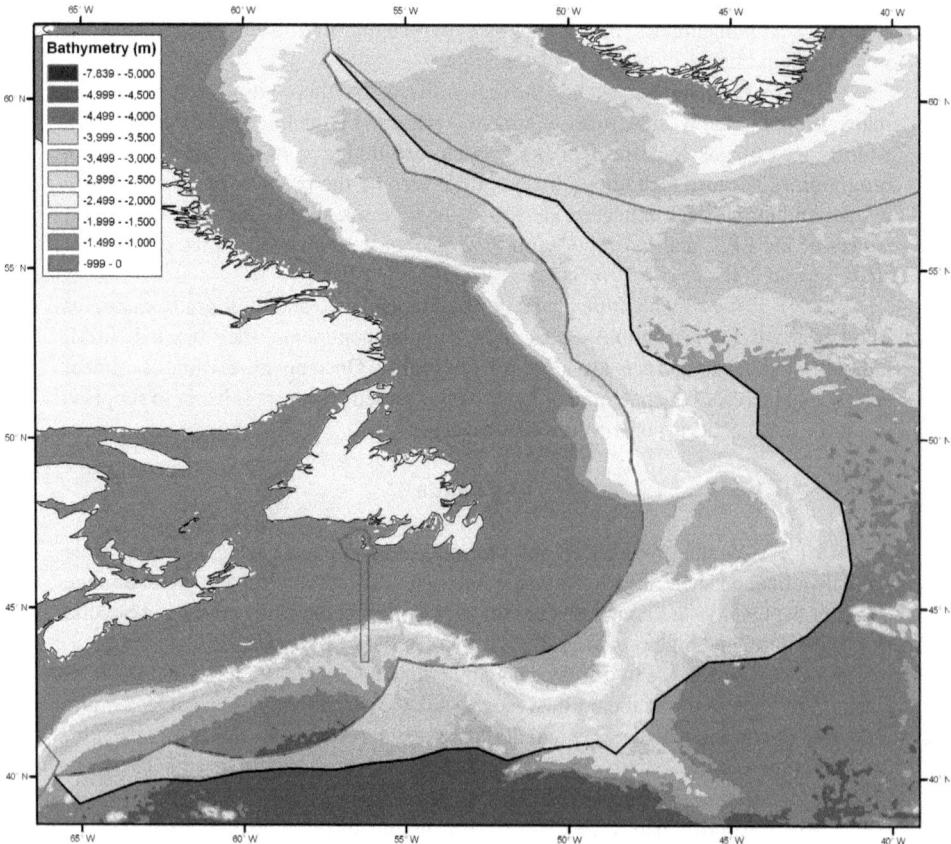

Figure 9. Potential Canadian Atlantic continental shelf claim area (in pale shading).

[43] The barrel of oil equivalent (BOE) is a unit of energy based on the approximate energy released by burning one barrel of crude oil.

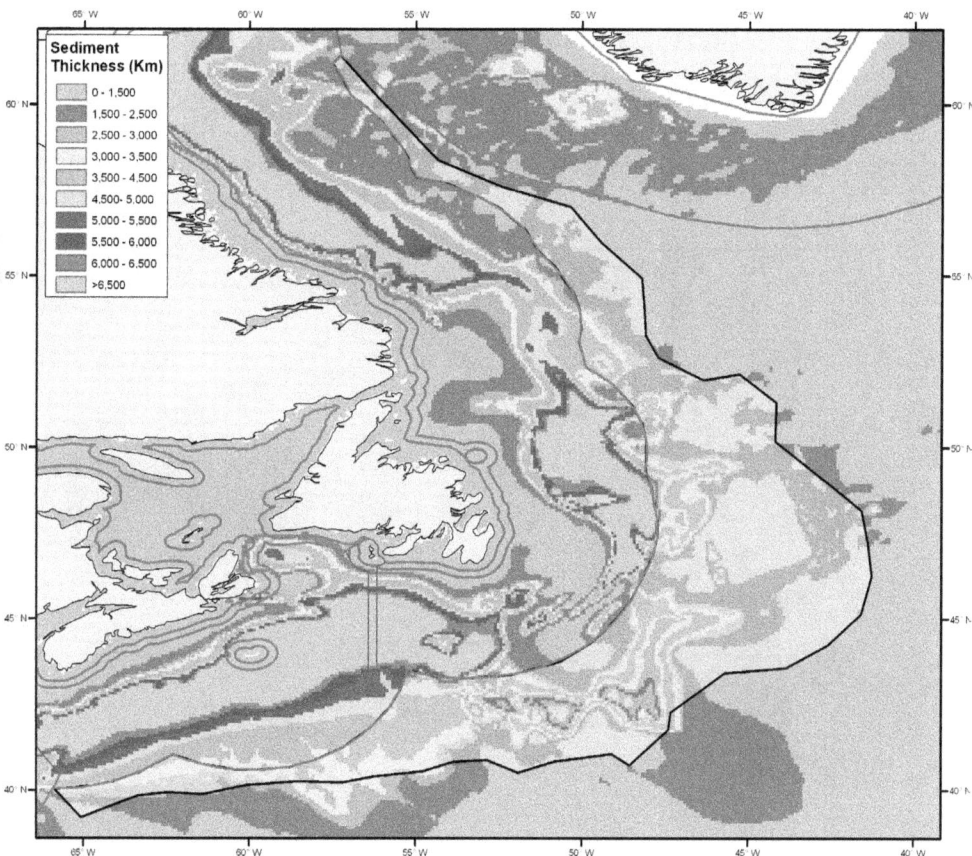

Figure 10. Potential OCS area for the Canadian Atlantic, including sediment thickness according to NGDC-modelled distribution (source http://www.ngdc.noaa.gov/mgg/sedthick/sedthick.html).

9.3.5   More than 256,700 sq km (33 per cent) of the potential Canadian Atlantic OCS has a sediment thickness of 3,000m or more. These areas may have some potential for hydrocarbon exploitation. Of this area, 66,700 sq km lie in water depths of less than 3,000m, and according to current technological capabilities, would be potentially exploitable.

9.3.6   In the Arctic Ocean, the potential Canadian OCS is estimated as covering 531,800 sq km (source: Canadian Geological Survey), but this may be an underestimate, and information regarding outer limit targets is not readily available. Canada ratified the Convention in 2003, and therefore has until 2013 to make its submission to the CLCS. The surveying to acquire suitable data to support its submission and preparation timelines reflects this schedule, and little information about its extent is available. Figure 10 illustrates this coverage, but it is likely that the total resource potential within the OCS is much greater than this.

9.3.7   An area of over 124,400 sq km within the Canadian Arctic OCS has a sediment thickness of 3,000m or more.[44] This figure represents 23 per cent of the potential OCS. Most recent publications notably that of the United States Geological Survey[45] suggest that the vast majority of hydrocarbon potential exists well within 200M EEZ limits, rather than in the OCS, although much interest has been raised recently regarding the ultra-deep water potential of these high latitude regions.[46]

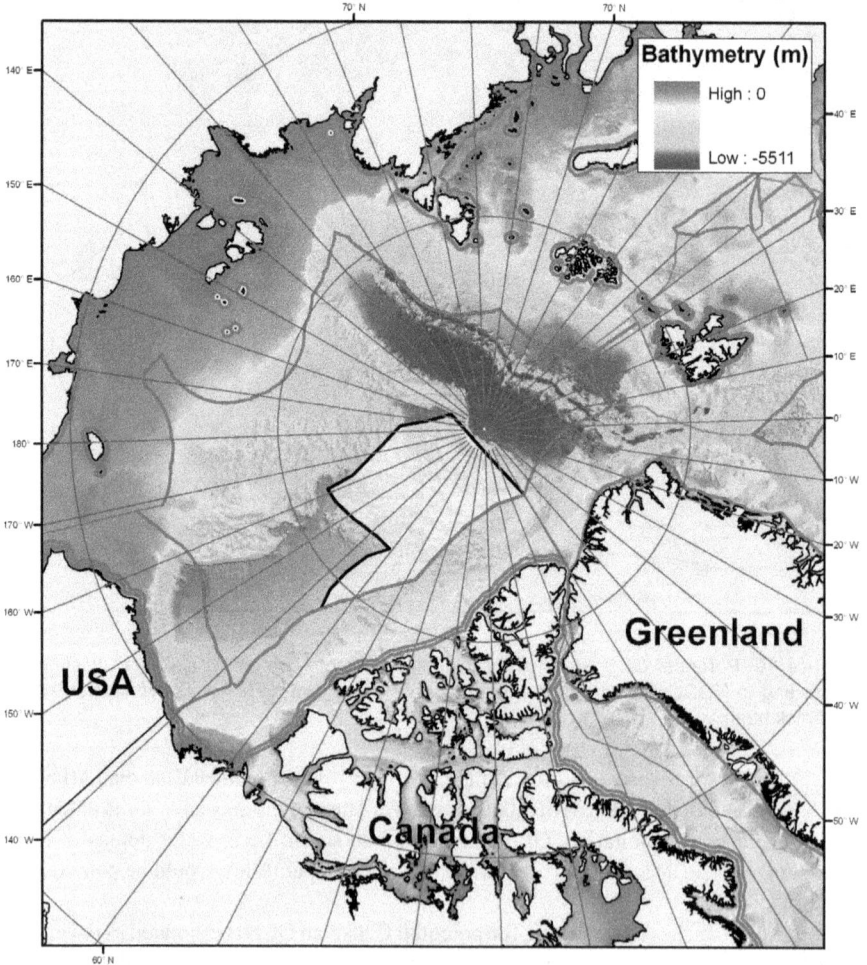

Figure 11. Potential Canadian Arctic OCS area (source: Canadian Geological Survey - http://www.gsc.nrcan.gc.ca/org/atlantic/unclos_e.php).

---

[44] According to modelled sediment thickness – source www.ngdc.noaa.gov/mgg/sedthick/sedthick.html.
[45] http://pubs.usgs.gov/fs/2008/3049/fs2008-3049.pdf.
[46] See section 3.2, above and footnote 26, for reference.

9.4 Sri Lanka

9.4.1   Sri Lanka is situated in the southwestern part of the Bay of Bengal, a significant region of the northeastern Indian Ocean dominated physiographically and geologically by the world's largest submarine sedimentary feature, the Bengal Fan. This extends over 1.4 million sq km of the Indian Ocean and is composed of sediments that originate mainly from the Ganges River. The Bengal Fan is about 3,000km long, and about 1,000km wide, and it has a maximum sedimentary thickness in the north of approximately 16.5 km. At the initiative of Sri Lanka, the Third United Nations Conference on the Law of the Sea adopted in Annex II of the Final Act special provisions

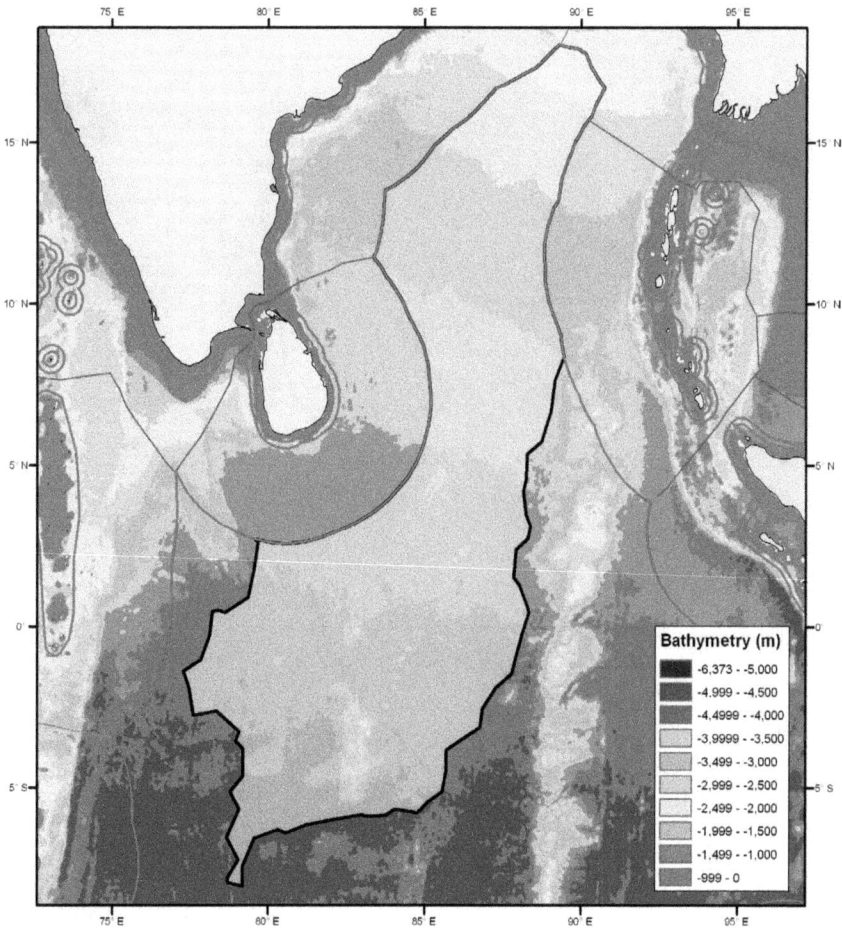

Figure 12. Predicted bathymetry and outline of the Sri Lankan OCS submission area in the Bay of Bengal.

applicable to the establishment of the outer edge of the continental margins in the southern part of the Bay of Bengal. These special provisions were developed because it was recognised that, if Article 76, and in particular paragraph 4(a)(i) and (ii) were to be applied, the characteristics of the sedimentary rocks would have resulted unfairly in a relatively limited juridical shelf excluding more than half of the margin. Annex II defines two circumstances which must prevail for the special provisions to apply: firstly, that the 200m isobath occurs at no more than 20M from a State's baselines and secondly, that the greater proportion of the sedimentary rock of the continental margin

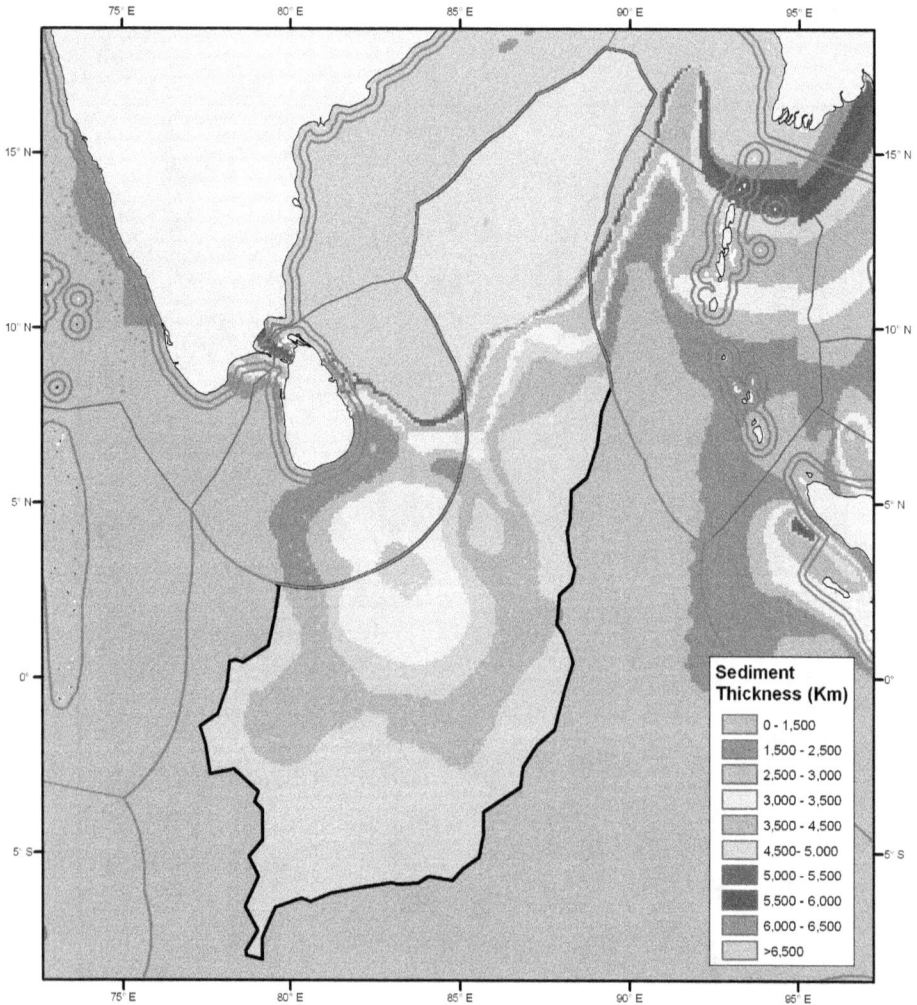

Figure 13. Outline of the Sri Lankan OCS submission area in the Bay of Bengal. Sediment thickness is shown according to NGDC-modelled distribution (source: www.ngdc.noaa.gov/mgg/sedthick/sedthick.html).

lies beneath the continental rise. To make allowance for the disadvantage that might result from application of Article 76, the special agreement provides that the outer limit of the continental margin may join points where the thickness of sediment is not less than 1 kilometre.

9.4.2   Published literature (including Curray et al., 2003), has allowed many commentators to suggest that as a result of these provisions, possible continental shelves could extend to cover much of the Bengal Fan area. The total area of this schematic coverage could be well over 1 million sq km (see Figure 12, derived from information provided by Sri Lanka in its submission on 8 May 2009). More than 290,200 sq km within the continental shelf beyond 200M has a sediment thickness of 3,000m or more, suggesting sufficient sediment overburden to allow the development of a petroleum system, although due to the steep edge to the Sri Lankan continental margin, all of the potential continental shelf beyond 200M lies in water depths in excess of 3,000m, which may increase the difficulties associated with oil or gas field development.

9.4.3   Sri Lanka is overwhelmingly dependent on petroleum (82 per cent). Most of South Asia is already grappling with energy shortfalls, typically in the form of recurrent, costly, and widespread electricity outages. Because of the economic and political ramifications arising from such shortfalls, improving the supply of energy, and particularly the supply of electricity, is an important priority of national and local governments. The countries of South Asia are looking to diversify their traditional energy supplies, promote additional foreign investment for energy infrastructure development, improve energy efficiency, reform and privatize energy sectors, and promote and expand regional energy trade and investment.

9.4.4   Growing demand for transportation fuels and industrial power has been a major factor behind the recent growth in South Asian oil consumption. In July 2003, the Sri Lankan Government approved the Petroleum Resources Act to allow private and foreign investment in its offshore oil and gas fields. In Sri Lanka, where oil is the dominant source of energy, oil consumption roughly doubled between 1991 and 2000. In 2002, Sri Lanka's oil consumption was 75,000 barrels per day. Sri Lanka imports all of its crude oil and uses it largely for electricity generation and transportation. The country has a refining capacity of 50,000 bbl/d. In recent years, it has further increased oil imports in an effort to avoid over-reliance on hydroelectricity.

9.4.5   If long-term projections of rapidly increasing gas demand in South Asia are correct, the region will require significant increases in production and/or imports. Even with expanded production, however, increased consumption of natural gas in South Asia is constrained by the region's inadequate domestic infrastructure. Gas imports would require the construction of either cross-border pipelines or liquefied natural gas (LNG) facilities, and success would also hinge on the successful construction of domestic gas pipeline infrastructure. A number of such infrastructure projects have been proposed in India and Pakistan.

9.5 Portugal

9.5.1   Portugal made a submission on 11 May 2009 in respect of its OCS areas beyond 200M. Its claim is based not only on the shelf areas to the west of the mainland, but also on deepwater areas surrounding the Azores island group (Figure 14). According to many observers, and as witnessed by submissions from other States with land territory associated with mid-ocean spreading ridges (such as Iceland, Norway, South Africa, Japan and the United Kingdom, Article 76 can be interpreted to provide for natural prolongation – and hence extension of the continental shelf – along such a ridge.

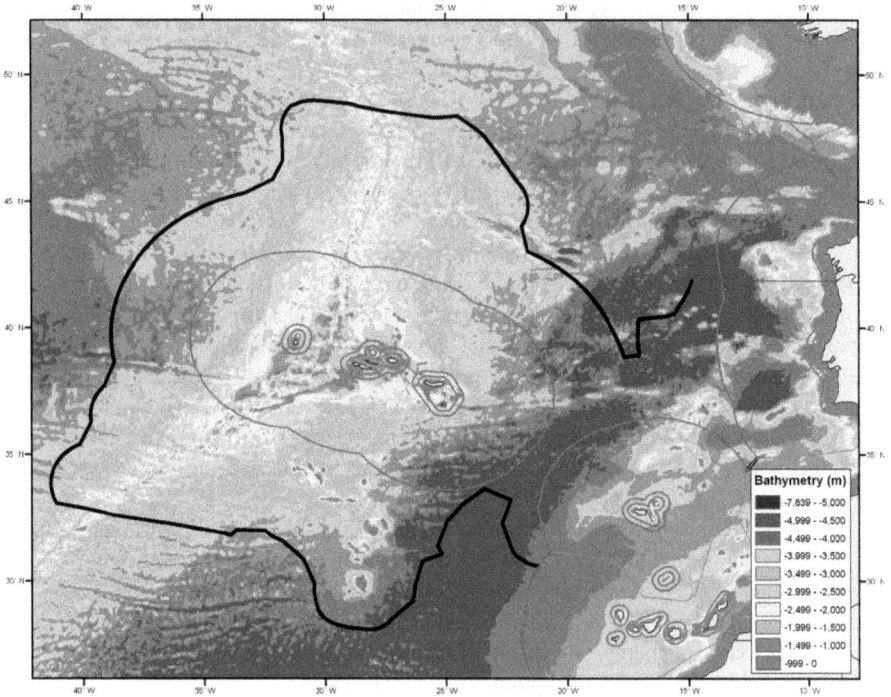

Figure 14. Map illustrating the area of OCS submitted by Portugal, 11 May 2009 (see http://www.un.org/Depts/los/clcs_new/submissions_files/prt44_09/prt2009executivesummary.pdf). This includes significant potential OCS along the MAR, North and South of Portugal's Azores Islands group.

9.5.2   The section of the Mid-Atlantic Ridge falling within Portugal's OCS submission in the region of the Azores has abundant and well documented, large-scale high temperature hydrothermal sites, each with potential for significant on-axis and off-axis polymetallic sulphide deposits.

9.5.3   The extremophile faunal assemblages[47] of the high temperature vent systems are also of interest to the pharmaceutical and biomedical industries. While wholescale

[47] Extremophile fauna are biota characterised by the ability to survive and propagate under extreme physical and chemical conditions; in this case, very high temperatures and pressures, and high concentrations of potentially toxic chemicals in the water mass.

development of this resource is far from mature, this field represents a growing and near-market resource, although not of direct significance to the implementation of Article 82.

9.5.4   Portugal's OCS submission includes both mainland and Azores Island group areas. As far as oil and gas production in the mainland OCS area is concerned, it should be noted that Portugal has good geological conditions for the formation and accumulation of hydrocarbons, both in conventional deposits and in the deep offshore. In fact, even though no commercially viable hydrocarbon accumulation has been found so far, the presence of liquid and gas hydrocarbons has been confirmed by several exploration drillings on and offshore.

9.5.5   Historically, hydrocarbon exploration in Portugal started onshore, mainly in the Lusitanian basin. In the 1970s, oil exploration took place in the outer offshore in less than 200m water depth. To date in Portugal, no exploration wells have been drilled bellow 500m water depth.

9.5.6   The Lusitanian sedimentary basin is underexplored, given that the number of wells per thousand kilometers was only 2.4, which is considered low. If we bear in mind that most of the wells in this basin were drilled onshore, with similar geological objectives, and that the majority did not reach prospective older layers, the low level of the evaluation of hydrocarbon potential becomes quite obvious.

10. CONCLUSION

10.1   While some coastal States are clearly well positioned and seemingly poised to move into the exploitation of conventional hydrocarbons in OCS areas without delay (see Table 1 above), it would be unwise to speculate too positively on such resource abundance beyond 200M. It is likely that OCS areas will largely lie outside the most prospective parts of a continental margin, and as such the resource potential will be modest, at best. Nonetheless, conventional oil and gas deposits will exist in OCS areas, and depending on market forces and technological requirements, may well form a significant part of certain coastal State's offshore resource base.

10.2   By contrast, methane hydrates are repeatedly quoted as a potential future source of natural gas, and deposits have either been proven or indicated in geophysical and geological data from the deep water sections of many continental margins. The technical challenges to extracting gas from within, or beneath the ice/gas deposits are still to be mastered, but there is no doubt that they will be. Predictions of when methane hydrate extraction will become commercial reality are undependable, but it will probably happen within 10-20 years, as conventional hydrocarbon reserves dwindle. As current estimates of methane in hydrates place them in both medium and deep water settings, they could form the most promising of all OCS deposits. The likely cost of production from systems that have yet to be developed can only be speculated upon, but is unlikely to be less than those for current oil and gas production, and this is likely to be a major factor in deductions before revenue calculation can be made.

10.3   The remaining non-living mineral deposits of any real potential for exploitation in OCS areas – polymetallic sulphides, manganese nodules and cobalt-rich ferromanganese crusts – are all long-term contenders as exploitable resources, but they are in the order of decades away from reaching an appropriate level of economic viability.

ANNEX I

NOTES ACCOMPANYING THE GLOBAL MAP OF CONTINENTAL SHELF AREAS IDENTIFIED IN SUBMISSIONS BY COASTAL STATES (AND ILLUSTRATED IN FIGURE 1) ACCORDING TO ARTICLE 76 OF THE UNITED NATIONS CONVENTION ON THE LAW OF THE SEA[1]

The outer limits of the continental shelf areas identified in the executive summaries of 51 submissions delivered to the Division for Ocean Affairs and the Law of the Sea (DOALOS)[2] at the United Nations as at 31 January 2010 have been digitally compiled and are illustrated in red on the accompanying map. The pale blue sections correspond to areas within 200M of States' baselines, many of which have been designated as EEZs under the LOS Convention.

In addition to the full continental shelf submissions received by DOALOS before 13 May 2009[3] (the deadline for 129 of the 160 Parties to the Convention), and one further submission made by Cuba on 1 June 2009, 44 additional sets of documentation were received in the form of preliminary information indicative of the potential outer limits of continental shelf invoking the special arrangements for, in particular, developing coastal States intending to make a submission but unable to meet the deadline.[4] Some of these additional areas are less precisely constrained than those in the full submissions, but summaries of these will be added to the current map as soon as practical. All documents relating to these cases are available at the DOALOS website.

The rationale behind all of the submissions lies in the provisions of Article 76 of the Convention, whereby coastal States demonstrating natural prolongation of land territory as submarine areas of their continental shelf can legally delineate these by outer limit points calculated on the basis of combinations of geomorphologic and geologic characteristics of the seafloor.[5]

Each of the cases submitted will be examined in the order that they were deposited at the United Nations by the CLCS, a body set up under the Convention and drawing on technical experts in marine geosciences from around the world. Once each case has been assessed for compliance with the provision of Article 76, the CLCS will issue recommendations regarding the outer limits of the shelf areas, and, following coastal States' acceptance of these recommendations, these can be established by the coastal State as final and binding.

The areas of OCS currently cover a total of approximately 23.8 million sq km. It is estimated that areas identified in the preliminary information documentation to date may cover a further area of several million sq km of continental shelf beyond 200M.

---

[1] www.un.org/Depts/los/convention_agreements/convention_overview_convention.htm.

[2] www.un.org/Depts/los/index.htm.

[3] www.un.org/Depts/los/clcs_new/commission_submissions.htm.

[4] http://www.un.org/Depts/los/clcs_new/commission_preliminary.htm.

[5] http://www.un.org/Depts/los/convention_agreements/texts/unclos/unclos_e.pdf.

These figures can be compared with estimates of approximately 70 million sq km of the world's oceans lying within 200M of coastal States' baselines.

Twenty-nine of the 159 States Parties that have ratified the Convention have a submission deadline of 10 years after their ratification date, although some of these have already delivered partial submissions, or preliminary indicative information, relating to continental shelf areas pending formal submissions.[6]

Of the 16 States that have yet to ratify the Convention, the USA undoubtedly has the largest potential continental shelf under Article 76 of UNLOSC, but the full extent of this can only be speculated upon at this point.

Many parts of the OCS are included in more than one submission, where neighbouring or adjacent States consider that their seafloor conditions make them each equally compliant with the criteria in UNLOSC used to define juridical continental shelf areas. Some of these overlap areas have resulted in the issuance of notes verbales to the United Nations, while others are the subject of mutual non-objection agreements, and others still have been resolved by means of a joint submission, presented by two or more coastal States.[7] These coordination initiatives will enable the CLCS to continue examining these cases, which would otherwise have to be halted, as the Commission has no mandate to work on submissions where a dispute exists.[8]

---

[6] http://www.un.org/Depts/los/reference_files/status2008.pdf.

[7] For example, joint submissions by: France, Ireland, Spain and the United Kingdom; Seychelles and Mauritius; and France and South Africa.

[8] Article 9 of Annex II of the Convention (see footnote 1).

ANNEX II

PART VI OF THE UNITED NATIONS CONVENTION ON THE LAW OF THE SEA: CONTINENTAL SHELF

Article 76
Definition of the continental shelf

1.   The continental shelf of a coastal State comprises the seabed and subsoil of the submarine areas that extend beyond its territorial sea throughout the natural prolongation of its land territory to the outer edge of the continental margin, or to a distance of 200 nautical miles from the baselines from which the breadth of the territorial sea is measured where the outer edge of the continental margin does not extend up to that distance.

2.   The continental shelf of a coastal State shall not extend beyond the limits provided for in paragraphs 4 to 6.

3.   The continental margin comprises the submerged prolongation of the land mass of the coastal State, and consists of the seabed and subsoil of the shelf, the slope and the rise. It does not include the deep ocean floor with its oceanic ridges or the subsoil thereof.

4.   (a) For the purposes of this Convention, the coastal State shall establish the outer edge of the continental margin wherever the margin extends beyond 200 nautical miles from the baselines from which the breadth of the territorial sea is measured, by either:

> (i)   a line delineated in accordance with paragraph 7 by reference to the outermost fixed points at each of which the thickness of sedimentary rocks is at least 1 per cent of the shortest distance from such point to the foot of the continental slope; or
>
> (ii) a line delineated in accordance with paragraph 7 by reference to fixed points not more than 60 nautical miles from the foot of the continental slope.
>
> (b) In the absence of evidence to the contrary, the foot of the continental slope shall be determined as the point of maximum change in the gradient at its base.

5.   The fixed points comprising the line of the outer limits of the continental shelf on the seabed, drawn in accordance with paragraph 4 (a) (i) and (ii), either shall not exceed 350 nautical miles from the baselines from which the breadth of the territorial sea is measured or shall not exceed 100 nautical miles from the 2,500 metre isobath, which is a line connecting the depth of 2,500 metres.

6.   Notwithstanding the provisions of paragraph 5, on submarine ridges, the outer limit of the continental shelf shall not exceed 350 nautical miles from the baselines from which the breadth of the territorial sea is measured. This paragraph does not apply to submarine elevations that are natural components of the continental margin, such as its plateaux, rises, caps, banks and spurs.

7.   The coastal State shall delineate the outer limits of its continental shelf, where that shelf extends beyond 200 nautical miles from the baselines from which the breadth of the territorial sea is measured, by straight lines not exceeding 60 nautical miles in length, connecting fixed points, defined by co-ordinates of latitude and longitude.

8.   Information on the limits of the continental shelf beyond 200 nautical miles from the baselines from which the breadth of the territorial sea is measured shall be submitted by the coastal State to the Commission on the Limits of the Continental Shelf set up under Annex II on the basis of equitable geographical representation. The Commission shall make recommendations to coastal States on matters related to the establishment of the outer limits of their continental shelf. The limits of the shelf established by a coastal State on the basis of these recommendations shall be final and binding.

9.   The coastal State shall deposit with the Secretary-General of the United Nations charts and relevant information, including geodetic data, permanently describing the outer limits of its continental shelf. The Secretary-General shall give due publicity thereto.

10. The provisions of this article are without prejudice to the question of delimitation of the continental shelf between States with opposite or adjacent coasts.

Article 77
Rights of the coastal State over the continental shelf

1.   The coastal State exercises over the continental shelf sovereign rights for the purpose of exploring it and exploiting its natural resources.

2.   The rights referred to in paragraph 1 are exclusive in the sense that if the coastal State does not explore the continental shelf or exploit its natural resources, no one may undertake these activities without the express consent of the coastal State.

3.   The rights of the coastal State over the continental shelf do not depend on occupation, effective or notional, or on any express proclamation.

4.   The natural resources referred to in this Part consist of the mineral and other non-living resources of the seabed and subsoil together with living organisms belonging to sedentary species, that is to say, organisms which, at the harvestable stage, either are immobile on or under the seabed or are unable to move except in constant physical contact with the seabed or the subsoil.

Article 78
*Legal status of the superjacent waters and air space and the rights
and freedoms of other States*

1.   The rights of the coastal State over the continental shelf do not affect the legal status of the superjacent waters or of the air space above those waters.

2.   The exercise of the rights of the coastal State over the continental shelf must not infringe or result in any unjustifiable interference with navigation and other rights and freedoms of other States as provided for in this Convention.

Article 79
Submarine cables and pipelines on the continental shelf

1.   All States are entitled to lay submarine cables and pipelines on the continental shelf, in accordance with the provisions of this article.

2.   Subject to its right to take reasonable measures for the exploration of the continental shelf, the exploitation of its natural resources and the prevention, reduction

and control of pollution from pipelines, the coastal State may not impede the laying or maintenance of such cables or pipelines.

3.   The delineation of the course for the laying of such pipelines on the continental shelf is subject to the consent of the coastal State.

4.   Nothing in this Part affects the right of the coastal State to establish conditions for cables or pipelines entering its territory or territorial sea, or its jurisdiction over cables and pipelines constructed or used in connection with the exploration of its continental shelf or exploitation of its resources or the operations of artificial islands, installations and structures under its jurisdiction.

5.   When laying submarine cables or pipelines, States shall have due regard to cables or pipelines already in position. In particular, possibilities of repairing existing cables or pipelines shall not be prejudiced.

Article 80
Artificial islands, installations and structures on the continental shelf

Article 60 applies *mutatis mutandis* to artificial islands, installations and structures on the continental shelf.

Article 81
Drilling on the continental shelf

The coastal State shall have the exclusive right to authorize and regulate drilling on the continental shelf for all purposes.

Article 82
Payments and contributions with respect to the exploitation of the
continental shelf beyond 200 nautical miles

1.   The coastal State shall make payments or contributions in kind in respect of the exploitation of the non-living resources of the continental shelf beyond 200 nautical miles from the baselines from which the breadth of the territorial sea is measured.

2.   The payments and contributions shall be made annually with respect to all production at a site after the first five years of production at that site. For the sixth year, the rate of payment or contribution shall be 1 per cent of the value or volume of production at the site. The rate shall increase by 1 per cent for each subsequent year until the twelfth year and shall remain at 7 per cent thereafter. Production does not include resources used in connection with exploitation.

3.   A developing State which is a net importer of a mineral resource produced from its continental shelf is exempt from making such payments or contributions in respect of that mineral resource.

4.   The payments or contributions shall be made through the Authority, which shall distribute them to States Parties to this Convention, on the basis of equitable sharing criteria, taking into account the interests and needs of developing States, particularly the least developed and the land-locked among them.

Article 83
Delimitation of the continental shelf between States with opposite or adjacent coasts

1.   The delimitation of the continental shelf between States with opposite or adjacent coasts shall be effected by agreement on the basis of international law, as referred to in Article 38 of the Statute of the International Court of Justice, in order to achieve an equitable solution.

2.   If no agreement can be reached within a reasonable period of time, the States concerned shall resort to the procedures provided for in Part XV.

3.   Pending agreement as provided for in paragraph 1, the States concerned, in a spirit of understanding and co-operation, shall make every effort to enter into provisional arrangements of a practical nature and, during this transitional period, not to jeopardize or hamper the reaching of the final agreement. Such arrangements shall be without prejudice to the final delimitation.

4.   Where there is an agreement in force between the States concerned, questions relating to the delimitation of the continental shelf shall be determined in accordance with the provisions of that agreement.

Article 84
Charts and lists of geographical co-ordinates

1.   Subject to this Part, the outer limit lines of the continental shelf and the lines of delimitation drawn in accordance with article 83 shall be shown on charts of a scale or scales adequate for ascertaining their position. Where appropriate, lists of geographical co-ordinates of points, specifying the geodetic datum, may be substituted for such outer limit lines or lines of delimitation.

2.   The coastal State shall give due publicity to such charts or lists of geographical co-ordinates and shall deposit a copy of each such chart or list with the Secretary-General of the United Nations and, in the case of those showing the outer limit lines of the continental shelf, with the Secretary-General of the Authority.

Article 85
Tunnelling

This Part does not prejudice the right of the coastal State to exploit the subsoil by means of tunnelling, irrespective of the depth of water above the subsoil.

ANNEX III

LIST OF PARTICIPANTS AT THE SEMINAR ON ISSUES ASSOCIATED WITH THE IMPLEMENTATION OF ARTICLE 82 OF THE UNITED NATIONS CONVENTION ON THE LAW OF THE SEA

Chatham House, London
11 – 13 February 2009

Invited Participants

Mr David Anderson
7 Onslow Crescent
Chislehurst
Kent, BR7 5RW
United Kingdom

D.H.Anderson@btinternet.com

Mr J.P. Andrews
Canada-Newfoundland and Labrador Offshore
  Petroleum Board
5th Floor, TD Place
140 Water Street
St. John's, NL
Canada A1C 6H6

jandrews@cnlopb.nl.ca

Mr Paul Barnes
Manager – Atlantic Canada
Canadian Association of Petroleum Producers
403, 235 Water Street
St. John's, NL
Canada, A1C 1BC

barnes@capp.ca

Professor Arne Bjorlykke
Geological Survey of Norway
NO-7491 Trondheim
Norway

arne.bjorlykke@ngu.no

Mr Gritakumar E. Chitty
14/1 Cambridge Place
Colombo 7
Sri Lanka

gechitty@gmail.com

Mr Tim Daniel
Edwards, Angell, Palmer & Dodge
1 Fetter Lane
London, EC4A 1JB

TDaniel@eapdlaw.com

Ambassador Hasjim Djalal
Jalan Kemang IV, No. 10A
Jakarta Selatan
Indonesia

hdh@cbn.net.id

Dr David Freestone
Lobingier Visiting Professor of Comparative
  Law and Jurisprudence
The George Washington University Law School
2000 H St NW
Washington DC 20052

dfreestone@law.gwu.edu

Dr Kaiser Gonçalves de Souza
Chief, Division of Marine Geology
Geological Survey of Brazil (CPRM)
Ministry of Mines and Energy
Headquarters: SGAN 603
Conj. J, Parte A, 1st floor
70.830-030 – Brasília – DF

Kaisers@df.cprm.gov.br

Professor Dr Gao Zhiguo
Director General
China Institute of Marine Affairs
State Oceanic Administration
1 Fuxingmenwai Avenue
Beijing 100860
The People's Republic of China

zgao@cima.gov.cn

Mr Huang Baoguang
Consulting Manager, Legal Department
China National Offshore Oil Corporation
P.O. Box 4705
No. 25 Chao Yang Men North Street
Dongcheng District
Beijing 100010
The People's Republic of China

huangbg@cnooc.com.cn

Mr Paul L. Kelly
Energy & Ocean Policy Consultant
5555 Del Monte Drive, Suite T-23
Houston, Texas 77056
U.S.A

paullkelly@aol.com

Professor Keyuan Zou
Harris Professor of International Law
Lancashire Law School
University of Central Lancashire
Preston, United Kingdom PR1 2HE

KZou@uclan.ac.uk

Professor Ted L. McDorman
University of Victoria
Faculty of Law
PO Box 2400 STN CSC
Victoria, British Columbia
Canada   V8W 3H7

tlmcdorm@uvic.ca

Ambassador Satya N. Nandan
New York
U.S.A.

Satya.n.nandan@gmail.com

Judge Dolliver Nelson
International Tribunal for the Law of the Sea
Hamburg, Germany

dnelson@btinternet.com

Mr David Ong
Reader in International & Environmental Law
University of Essex Law School
Wivenhoe Park, Colchester
Essex CO4 3SQ

daveo@essex.ac.uk

Dr Frida Armas Pfirter
Paraguay 1545
1061-Buenos Aires
Argentina

Frida_Armas@yahoo.com

Mr Mahmoud Ahmed Samir Samy
Minister Plenipotentiary
Deputy Assistant Minister of Foreign Affairs
Cairo, Egypt

mssamy@hotmail.com

Mr Walter De Sá Leitão
Av. Chile 65 ala 701 Centro
Rio de Janeiro
Brazil

saleitao@petrobras.com.br

Dr Rashid Sumaila
Fisheries Economics Research Unit
Fisheries Centre
University of British Columbia
2202 Main Mall,
Vancouver, B.C., V6T
Canada

r.sumaila@fisheries.ubc.ca

Professor Dr Rüdiger Wolfrum
Max Planck Institute for Comparative Public
   Law and International Law
Im Neuenheimer Feld 535
69120 Heidelberg
Germany

wolfrum@mpil.de

Dr Ibibia Lucky Worika
General Legal Counsel
Organization of Petroleum Exporting Countries
   (OPEC)
Obere Donaustrasse 93
A-1020 Vienna,
Austria

ilworika@opec.org

Resource personnel

Dr Lindsay Parson
National Oceanography Centre
University of Southampton
Waterfront Campus, European Way
Southampton SO14 3ZH
United Kingdom

L.Parson@noc.soton.ac.uk

Dr Aldo Chircop
Professor of Law
Marine & Environmental Law Institute
Dalhousie University
Halifax, NS, B3H 4H9
Canada

Aldo.Chircop@Dal.Ca

International Seabed Authority

Nii Allotey Odunton
Secretary-General

nodunton@isa.org.jm

Michael Lodge
Legal Adviser

mlodge@isa.org.jm

Kening Zhang
Senior Legal Officer

kzhang@isa.org.jm

Chatham House

Bernice Lee
Head, Energy, Environment and Development
Programme

blee@chathamhouse.org

Duncan Brack
Senior Research Fellow

dbrack@chathamhouse.org

Heike Baumüller
Senior Research Fellow

Cleo Paskal
Associate Fellow

me@cleopaskal.com

LITERATURE CITED

Agterberg, F.P. and Franklin, J.M., "Estimation of the probability of occurrence of polymetallic massive sulfide deposits on the ocean floor", in: P. Teleki et al. (eds.), *Marine Minerals*, Kluwer, 467-483 (1987).

Binns, R.A., et al., "Hydrothermal oxide and gold-rich sulfate deposits of Franklin Seamount, western Woodlark Basin, Papua New Guinea", 88(8) *Economic Geology*, 2122-2153 (1993).

Collett, T.S., "Potential of gas hydrates outlined", *Oil & Gas Journal*, June 22, 84-87 (1992).

Cook, P.J., and C.M. Carleton, *Continental Shelf Limits – The Scientific and Legal Interface* (Oxford University Press, 2000).

Curray, J., F.J. Emmel and D.G. Moore, "The Bengal Fan: morphology, geometry, stratigraphy, history and processes", *Marine and Petroleum Geology* 19, 1191-1223 (2003).

Gornitz, V. and I. Fung, "Potential distribution of methane hydrates in the world's oceans", v. 8, no. 3, *Global Biogeochemical Cycles*, 335-347 (1994).

Hannington, M.D. and S.D. Scott, "Gold and silver potential of polymetallic sulphide deposits on the sea floor", 7(3), *Marine Mining*, 271-285 (1988).

International Energy Agency, "Global Offshore Oil Prospects to 2000", IEA report, 120pp (1996).

International Law Association. Legal Issues of the Outer Continental Shelf. Proceedings of the Berlin Conference, 2004, http://www.ila-hq.org.

International Law Association. Legal Issues of the Outer Continental Shelf. Proceedings of the Toronto Conference, 2006, http://www.ila-hq.org.

International Seabed Authority, *Global Non-Living Resources on the Extended Continental Shelf: Prospects at the Year 2000*, Technical Study: No.1, Kingston, ISA (2001).

International Seabed Authority, *Issues associated with the Implementation of Article 82 of the United Nations Convention on the Law of the Sea*, Technical Study: No. 4, Kingston, ISA (2009).

Kendall Freeman, "Oil and gas deposits at international boundaries", 2007. Downloadable at http://www.eapdlaw.com/files/News/beea97f3-7544-42e1-be4d-00e1e25f9d2a/ Presentation/NewsAttachment/bf4112ae-d66c-4209-a623-06c8f8a3214c/Oil%20and%20 gas%20deposits%20at%20international%20boundaries%20-%20March%202007%20-%20 Kendall%20Freeman%20Guidance%20Note.pdf

Klett, T.R., et al., "Ranking of the world's oil and gas provinces by known petroleum volumes", U. S. Department of the Interior, U.S. Geological Survey, Open-File Report 97-463 (1997).

Krason, J. and P.D. Finley, "Messoyakh Gas Field - Russia: West Siberian Basin", *Amer. Assoc. Petrol. Geol., Treatise of Petroleum Geology, Atlas of Oil and Gas Fields, Structural Traps VII*, 197-220 (1992).

Kvenvolden, K.A., "Gas hydrates as a potential energy resource – a review of their methane content", in Howell, D.G., ed., *The future of energy gases*: U.S. Geological Survey Professional Paper 1570, 555-561 (1993).

Kvenvolden, K.A., G.D. Ginsburg, and V.A. Soloviev, "Worldwide distribution of subaquatic gas hydrates", 13(1), *Geo-Marine Letters*, 32-40 (1993).

Lee, M.W., et al., "Seismic character of gas hydrates on the southeastern U.S. continental margin", 16, *Marine Geophys. Res.*, 163-184 (1994).

Li, Y., *Transfer of technology for deep sea-bed mining: the 1982 Law of the Sea Convention and beyond*, Nijhoff, (2005).

Makogon, Y.F., et al., "Detection of a pool of natural gas in a solid hydrate state", 196/1, *Doklady Akademii Nauk SSSR*, 197-200 (1971).

Makogon, Y.F., "Production from natural gas hydrate deposits", 10, *Gazovaya Promishlennost*, 24-26 (1984).

Max, M.D., "Gas hydrate and acoustically laminated sediments: potential environment cause of anomalously low acoustic bottom loss in deep-ocean sediments", U.S. Naval Research Laboratory, NRL Report 9235, 68pp (1990).

McDorman, T.L., "The Continental Shelf Beyond 200 miles: Law and Politics in the Arctic Ocean", in *The World Ocean in Globalization: Challenges for Marine Regions*, Fridtjof Nansen Institute, Oslo, 21-23 August 2008.

McIver, R.D., "Gas hydrates", in Meyer, R.F. and J.C. Olson (eds.), *Long-term Energy Resources*, Pitman, Boston, 713-726 (1981).

Miles, P.R., "Potential distribution of methane hydrate beneath the European continental margins", 22/23, *Geophysical Research Let.*, 3179-3182 (1995).

Morgan, C.L., "Resource estimates of the Clarion-Clipperton manganese nodule deposits", in Cronan D.S. (ed.), *Handbook of Marine Mineral Deposits*, CRC press, 145-170 (2000).

Moss, R., Scott, S.D. and R.A. Binns, "Concentrations of gold and other ore metals in volcanics hosting the PACMANUS seafloor sulphide deposit", *13 JAMSTEC Journal of Deep Sea Research*, 257-267 (1997).

Nandan, S.N., Rosenne, S. and N.R. Grandy. (eds), *Second Committee: Articles 1 to 85, Annexes l and ll, and Final Act, Annex l,* Center for Oceans Law and Policy, University of Virginia School of Law, Commentary, 1040 (1993).

Nordquist, M.H., Moore, J.N, and T.H. Heidar, *Legal and scientific aspects of continental shelf limits*, Center for Oceans Law and Policy, University of Virginia School of Law, Martinus Nijhoff Publishers (2004).

Prensky, S.E., "A review of gas hydrates and formation evaluation of hydrate-bearing reservoirs" (paper GGG), presented at 1995 meeting of the Society of Professional Well Log Analysts, Paris, France, June 26-29, 1995.

Prescott, J.R.V., *The Maritime Political Boundaries of the World*, Methuen & Co, London, 1985.

Prescott, J.R.V., and C. Schofield, *The Maritime Political Boundaries of the World* (2nd edition), Leiden (2005).

United Nations, A/CONF.62/C.2/L.98/Add.1, map illustrating various formulae for the definition of the continental shelf, Reports of the Third Conference on the Law of the Sea.

United Nations Convention on the Law of the Sea, Montego Bay, 10 December 1982, 1833, *U.N.T.S. 3.*

United Nations Convention on the Law of the Sea, CLCS/11, Scientific and Technical Guidelines of the Commission on the Limits of the Continental Shelf, 13 May 1999.

United Nations Environment Programme, "Ecosystems and biodiversity in deep waters and high seas", *UNEP Regional Seas Reports and Studies No 178*, UNEP/IUCN, Switzerland (2006).

www.ingramcontent.com/pod-product-compliance
Lightning Source LLC
Chambersburg PA
CBHW060641210326
41520CB00010B/1699